JOAN MIRÓ

Joan Miró. September 1956. Photo André Ostier

JOAN MIRÓ

BY JAMES THRALL SOBY

The Museum of Modern Art, New York

Distributed by Doubleday & Company, Inc., Garden City, New York

Published by the Museum of Modern Art, New York, 1959

All rights reserved

Library of Congress Catalogue Card Number 59–10311

Typography by Susan Draper

Printed in Germany by Brüder Hartmann, Berlin

CONTENTS

ACKNOWLEDGMENTS   4

JOAN MIRÓ by James Thrall Soby   7

NOTES TO THE TEXT   149

LIST OF EXHIBITIONS   151

BIBLIOGRAPHY by Bernard Karpel   153

INDEX   162

ACKNOWLEDGMENTS

In the preparation of this book I am first of all indebted to the artist himself, who has been most helpful and kind in replying to the many requests for information I have had to send him. Miró's New York dealer and friend for many years, Pierre Matisse, has assisted with research in every way possible, and so has Mrs. Matisse.

Alfred H. Barr, Jr., Monroe Wheeler, and William S. Liebermann have made important editorial suggestions as to the text which follows. The last-named in particular, Director of the Museum's Miró exhibition on which this book is partly based, has given valuable help and has made available his own extensive documents on the artist's career to date, many of them supplied by Aimé Maeght, Miró's Paris dealer, and Jacques Dupin, whose monograph on the artist is soon to be published.

Alicia Legg, of the Department of Painting and Sculpture, has worked on the exhibition and book with her usual care and skill, with estimable help from Edith Herman of the Print Department. The Publications Department's Frances Pernas has planned this publication with energy and patience, and has been ably assisted by Susan Draper.

Special thanks are due to Dorothy Dudley and David Vance of the Registrar's office who, under extraordinary pressures of circumstance, managed to bring Miró's *The Farm* from Havana during times of civil strife, with the valuable aid of Francis J. Donahue of the American Embassy in Cuba, the personnel of the National Airlines, and Sergio Lopez Mesa of the Institute of National Culture in Cuba. I am indebted, too, to Ernest Hemingway, owner of this masterwork of Miró's early career, for letting us borrow his irreplaceable picture; he also put up sympathetically with my constant phone interruptions while he was on vacation.

Anne Jones, Vice-Chairman of the Museum's Junior Council, assembled extensive files of Miró's works in American collections; Helen Franc devised the method of research which unearthed the British prototype of Miró's *Portrait of Mrs. Mills in 1750*. Joan Prats, a lifelong friend of Miró, was helpful in sending photographs from Barcelona, and so was José Maria Gudiol Ricart. Pierre Loeb, who gave Miró his first one-man show in Paris, has supplied useful facts about the artist's career, as has José Luis Sert, co-architect of the Spanish Pavilion at the Paris Exposition of 1937, where Miró's large mural, *The Reaper*, was shown as well as Picasso's *Guernica*. The most difficult translations from the French in the present text are the thoughtful work of Sheila La Farge. The color photography is mostly the work of Frank Lerner. The transparency of the Cincinnati mural was supplied by Skidmore, Owings & Merrill, architects for the hotel in which the mural hangs.

Finally, for special assistance given us, our deepest thanks are due the following friends of the Museum: Mr. and Mrs. James W. Alsdorf; Mr. and Mrs. Armand P. Bartos; Mr. and Mrs. Gordon Bunshaft; Mr. and Mrs. Ralph F. Colin; M. and Mme Raoul Lévy; Mr. and Mrs. Samuel A. Marx; Mr. and Mrs. Pierre Matisse; Mr. and Mrs. Morton G. Neumann; Mr. and Mrs. Neils Onstad; Mr. and Mrs. Duncan Phillips; Nelson A. Rockefeller; Mr. and Mrs. Joseph Slifka; Eugene Victor Thaw; Mr. and Mrs. Richard K. Weil.

JAMES THRALL SOBY

In the captions to the illustrations the date is enclosed in parentheses when it does not appear on the work.

JOAN MIRÓ

"It is difficult for me to speak of my painting, for it is always born in a state of hallucination, provoked by some shock or other, objective or subjective, for which I am entirely irresponsible."[1] This statement by Joan Miró was published as long ago as 1933, and would undoubtedly be revised now that Surrealism's fevers have subsided in his mind. Indeed, in 1948 he said to James Johnson Sweeney: "Nowadays I rarely start a picture from an hallucination, as I did in the twenties, or, as later, from collages. What is most interesting to me today is the material I am working with. It supplies the shock which suggests the form just as cracks in a wall suggested shapes to Leonardo."[2] Nevertheless, there is a decided quality of trance in many of Miró's works, an impetuous spontaneity and innocence which make him one of the freshest and most beguiling painters of our time.

Miró is the most instinctively talented artist of his generation, his poetic invention unflagging. His achievement is the more impressive in that he was born so soon after his great countryman, Picasso—twelve years, to be exact, the precise interval which separates Picasso's birthdate from that of another major artist, Henri Matisse. It is difficult to follow thus quickly in the wake of a giant, without benefit of the calming lull or shifting storm which comes after a full generation has passed. But Miró, like Picasso, has furthered in a new and valid direction the art of his predecessor, a fact which his countryman has openly acknowledged.

Joan Miró was born in Montroig, a small town near Barcelona, on April 20, 1893. His Catalan heritage has been of overwhelming importance for his career, and no other sources of inspiration have been quite as central as his native province's Romanesque frescoes, its music, its dances, and festivals. Perhaps only Miró could say with such pride, "In Barcelona I paint in the room where I was born."[3] In contrast to Picasso and Gris, both deliberate expatriates whose mature careers unfolded in France, Miró, though he worked in Paris for a number of years, has a profound need of the

Modesto Urgell (1840–1919): *Twilight*. Collection José Maria Gudiol Ricart, Barcelona

environment in which he was born and grew up. Since World War II he has lived in Spain, first in Palma de Mallorca, later in Barcelona, and now again in Palma.

The Catalan landscape has engaged him persistently. "The vigorous Catalan landscape," he once said, "without any trace of anecdotal description, has been a capital element of my plastic and poetic conception."⁴ His passionate regard for details of local terrain could scarcely be more acutely summarized than by an anecdote recounted by his collaborator in making ceramics, Artigas: "When Miró first arrived at Gallifa [a tiny village thirty miles from Barcelona], he was very excited by the great rocks all around. He went out and began painting on them directly, just for his own pleasure [see page 134]."⁵

STUDENT YEARS

In 1907 Miró entered the School of Fine Arts in Barcelona. His first teacher there was Modesto Urgell Y Inglada (1839–1919), a Catalan painter unusually conversant with the French tradition, who had lived for long periods in Paris and come under the varying influences of Courbet, Millet, Daubigny, and Böcklin. Urgell himself was noted for his romantic landscapes and fond of such aspects of nature as waterfalls, lonely cemeteries, and deserted vistas. He seems also to have had a passion for economy of pictorial and technical means, a fact which even then may have endeared him to the youthful Miró.

At any rate, to this day Miró speaks of Urgell with affection and gratitude. In a recent letter to the writer he declared: "Modesto Urgell, my first teacher, exercised a great influence on me through his sentiment of solitude and *dépouillement* which still exist in my own work." And elsewhere he has said: "Even today I recognize forms constantly appearing in my work that originally impressed me in his [Urgell's] painting, though it is true that Urgell was a romantic follower of Böcklin and saw things in a sad light while these forms in my work always take a gay character. I remember two paintings of Urgell in particular, both characterized by long, straight, twilit horizons which cut the pictures in halves: one a painting of a moon above a cypress tree, another with a crescent moon low in the sky. Three forms which have become an obsession with me represent the imprint of Urgell: a red circle, the moon and a star. They keep coming back, each time slightly different."[6] A glance at the Urgell painting here reproduced (opposite) will make clear what Miró means.

A second teacher at the Barcelona School of Fine Arts was José Pascó (1855–1910), whose principal contribution may have been the fact that he persuaded his young pupil to experiment. In Miró's words to the writer, "José Pascó urged me on and encouraged me to express myself with complete liberty." On the other hand, Pascó appears to have given his disciple a rigorous training in draftsmanship, and in his 1948 interview with James Sweeney, Miró declared: "Pascó was the other teacher whose influence I still feel... Color was easy for me. But with form I had great difficulty. Pascó taught me to draw from the sense of touch by giving me objects which I was not allowed to look at, but which I was afterwards made to draw. Even today ... the effect of this touch-drawing experience returns in my interest in sculpture: the need to mold with my hands, to pick up a ball of wet clay like a child and squeeze it. From this I get a physical satisfaction that I cannot get from drawing or painting..."[7] Considering the many fine drawings Miró has made during his career, it is difficult to believe that draftsmanship can have been a grave problem for long, though admittedly he has always been first and foremost a colorist.

In 1910 the artist's parents objected to his chosen career so strenuously that he was forced to withdraw from the School of Fine Arts and work as a clerk. Yet perhaps the parents cannot be blamed entirely for this interruption in Miró's schooling; one gathers that at the time he was himself rather discouraged with his progress. If so, his pessimism was short-lived. In 1912 he enrolled in the Academy Galí in Barcelona

The Peasant. (c. 1914). Oil on canvas.
25 ⁵/₈ × 19 ³/₄". Galerie Maeght, Paris

and resumed his studies. The director of the Academy, Francisco de Asís Galí (born 1880) was a younger man than Urgell and Pascó, and his Academy must have been much less strictly an art school than the School of Fine Arts. As Miró puts the matter in a letter to the writer, "Francisco de Asís Galí, in his Academy, apart from teaching us painting, at the same time enriched our spirit through music and poetry." Miró adds significantly: "This has always been my goal, to transcend the purely plastic fact to reach other horizons." We shall see later, in discussing Miró's career of the 1920s in Paris, how closely related he felt to poets and musicians and how much he was affected by their work. His lasting and important predilection for the other arts was undoubtedly first stimulated by Galí.

The Coffee Pot. (1916?). Oil on cardboard, 19⁵/₈×21⁵/₈″. Galerie Maeght, Paris

EARLY PAINTINGS

In 1915 Miró left the Academy Galí to paint by himself. For roughly two years his progress was eclectic and uncertain. His landscapes of the period and also his drawings show that he had become aware of the profound visual revolution which had begun with the post-impressionists and continued on through the Parisian fauves and the expressionists of Central Europe. There can be little doubt that among the post-impressionists Cézanne and van Gogh meant most to him, but their movement as a whole probably accounts for Miró's use of distortions and arbitrary color. In the

View of Montroig. (1917). Oil on cardboard, 26¹⁄₈×29″. Pierre Matisse Gallery, New York

View of Montroig. (1917). Oil on canvas, $23^1/_2 \times 28^5/_8$". Collection Mr. and Mrs. James W. Alsdorf, Winnetka, Illinois

relatively few pictures of 1915 and 1916 which have survived, one feels an intense sense of striving, a slow and valorous attempt to move out from the provincial shoals into the mainstream of contemporary painting. If Miró's paintings of this period can seldom be described as authoritative, they have at times a unique vigor and they prophesy, if only at intervals, the emergence of an idiosyncratic talent.

A turning point in Miró's career came when, in 1917, he met the Barcelona dealer, José Dalmau, a retired painter who had become a bellwether for the members of the vanguard in Catalan art. As early as 1912 in Barcelona Dalmau had organized an exhibition of the cubists, including Duchamp, Gleizes, Metzinger, and Léger, and it may well have been through him that Miró discovered that the fauves had been succeeded by even more advanced artists, especially the cubists. Nevertheless, Miró quite understandably clung for a time to the precepts learned during his solitary labors of 1915 and 1916. In his works of 1917 (pages 12, 13), we see a new structural discipline applied to his earlier, free arabesques of vivid and already personal color.

In 1917 Miró took perhaps his greatest stride forward in portraiture, as in the *Portrait of J. F. Rafols*, in which Cézanne's planar solidity is combined with a van Gogh-like ferocity. From this same year dates the remarkable *Portrait of E. C. Ricart* (opposite), a work which suggests that Miró was not unaware of Chagall's rainbow overlays of color and aggressive distortions. Yet the picture contains passages which are pure and mature Miró. Look, for example, at the handling of Ricart's hair, at the palette at the upper left, which holds its place against a dazzling yellow ground and is related in contour to forms in the artist's later abstractions. Or consider the way in which Miró has made telling use of the loops and seams on his model's pajama jacket. The signs of a highly gifted painter are already apparent. And since the subject is so seldom broached, a word must be said about Miró's psychological astuteness in portraiture. This rather neglected virtue of his art is unmistakably apparent in the *Portrait of a Goldsmith* (Ramón Sunyer) of 1918 (page 16). It is even more apparent in *The Chauffeur* (page 17), in which dignity combines with humility, defiance (the solemn derby hat) with pride. Moreover, the identifying image of an automobile on the wall brings to mind the artist's statement, "For me a form is never something abstract; it is always a sign of something. It is always a man, a bird, or something else. For me painting is never form for form's sake."[8]

Another capital painting of 1918 is the *Kitchen Garden with Donkey* (page 21), which foretells in many important respects *The Farm* of 1921–22, a masterwork of Miró's entire career. The picture's thoughtful stylizations, as in the symmetrical placing of

Portrait of E. C. Ricart. (1917). Oil and pasted paper on canvas, $31^7/_8 \times 25^3/_8''$. Collection Mr. and Mrs. Samuel A. Marx, Chicago

Portrait of a Goldsmith. 1918. Oil on canvas, 27 × 21″. Collection Mr. and Mrs. Sidney M. Shoenberg, St. Louis

The Chauffeur. 1918. Oil on canvas, $27^1/_2 \times 24^1/_2''$. Collection Edward A. Bragaline, New York

17

the flowers and shrubbery, its firm perspective and striated clouds, its curious amalgam of primitivism and extreme skill—these are the proofs that Miró had found his own, thoroughly Spanish conception of painting. He was to repeat the success of the *Kitchen Garden with Donkey* that same year in a second landscape called *View of a Farm* (page 20). In both paintings we are aware of that strange interplay between gaiety and pensive sobriety which is characteristic of a good part of the artist's work. In personal terms this characteristic is well symbolized by Jacques Viot's account of Miró dancing in a Montmartre café after the opening of his first Paris exhibition: "Not a slide nor a figure nor the least step were forgotten. The other dancers were brought to a standstill by so much conscience. And Miró ... continued his tango as if he had learned it in a book."[9]

By the end of 1918 Miró had completed a quite considerable body of work; his first one-man show, organized by José Dalmau early in the year (February 16-March 3) had contained sixty-four canvases and many drawings. The show seems to have had some local success, thanks in part to Dalmau's promotional skill but also on its own merits. And one assumes that Dalmau was already talking to his young protégé about the excitement of the Paris art scene (he was to arrange Miró's second one-man exhibition at the Galerie La Licorne, Paris, in 1921). As the war neared its end the painter became more and more determined to visit Paris and perhaps especially to see Picasso, whose family he knew in Barcelona, and whom he had apparently met personally during his student years at a performance of the Diaghilev ballet in Barcelona.

Opposite: *Standing Nude*. 1918. Oil on canvas, 60$^1/_8$ × 47$^1/_2$".
Collection Mr. and Mrs. Joseph Slifka, New York

Henri Matisse (1869–1954): *The Red Studio*. (1911). Oil on canvas, 71$^1/_4$ × 86$^1/_4$". The Museum of Modern Art, New York, Mrs. Simon Guggenheim Fund

19

View of a Farm. 1918. Oil on canvas, $25^1/_2 \times 31^3/_4''$. Collection Mr. and Mrs. James W. Alsdorf, Winnetka, Illinois

Kitchen Garden with Donkey. (1918). Oil on canvas. Private collection, New York

The Village of Montroig. 1919. Oil on canvas, $28^3/_4 \times 24''$. Collection Sra. Dolores Miró de Fernández, Palma de Mallorca

The Olive Grove. 1919. Oil on canvas, 28^1/$_2$ × 35^1/$_4$″. Collection Mr. and Mrs. Leigh B. Block, Chicago

THE FIRST TRIP TO PARIS

Miró arrived in Paris on March 3, 1919 and found lodgings at the Hôtel de la Victoire, rue Nôtre Dame des Victoires. He stayed there until the following spring, when his recurrent longing for Montroig took him home again for six months. Meanwhile, a great deal had happened to him. In a recent disgruntled interview with the painter by Edouard Roditi, Miró is quoted as having said: "When I first came to Paris, I felt that the Impressionists and Fauvism were both dead and that Cubism was already moribund. Only Dada seemed to me to be really alive."[10] It is difficult to believe in the account's accuracy, since not until roughly five years later did Miró's art show any consistent influence from the Dada movement. Moreover, in a letter of November 3, 1958 to the writer Miró declared: "As I told you, from 1916 to 1920 I was impassioned by van Gogh, Rousseau, and Picasso—admirations which I feel to this day in the highest degree."

It seems far more likely that Miró's horizons on his arrival in Paris were greatly extended by his visits with Picasso, who was never part of the Dada uprising, and who received Miró with a warmth of which the latter still speaks gratefully. As we all know, Picasso was and is not only a major painter but a connoisseur of extraordinary perception, and it may have been at his apartment that Miró first became aware of the miraculous gifts of an artist mentioned in his list of early favorites—the Douanier Rousseau. At any rate, Miró's own *Seated Nude* of 1919 (page 27) has much of Rousseau's enchanted naivete and directness. The picture's debt to cubism is also apparent in the faceted handling of the arms and upper torso. Yet however profound Miró's admiration for the cubists, he was not in his own word *"dérouté"* by them.[11] The

Young Girl. (1919?). Oil on paper, 13 × 11".
Collection Joan Prats, Barcelona

Still Life with Toy Horse. 1920. Oil on canvas, $32^1/_2 \times 29^1/_2$". Collection Mr. and Mrs. C. Earle Miller, Downingtown, Pennsylvania

Self Portrait. (1919). Oil on canvas.
Collection Pablo Picasso, Vauvenargues,
France

Seated Nude with its shimmering pink tonality, is in no sense a mere school piece nor
is the image dominated by its cubistic passages. These passages are held in subtle
balance with the straightforward painting of the head (a whole chapter could be written
about Miró's original and penetrating stylizations of human hair), of the needlepoint
cushion and striped rug.

Considering that Miró's color has always been so unmistakably Spanish, his self-
avowed debt to Henri Matisse, a Frenchman to his fingertips, seems at first a trifle
puzzling. What more specific than a certain audacity did Miró owe Matisse, whose
influence he had obviously felt in the *Standing Nude* of 1918 (page 18). The writer
asked Miró this question some years ago, and his reply was something like this:

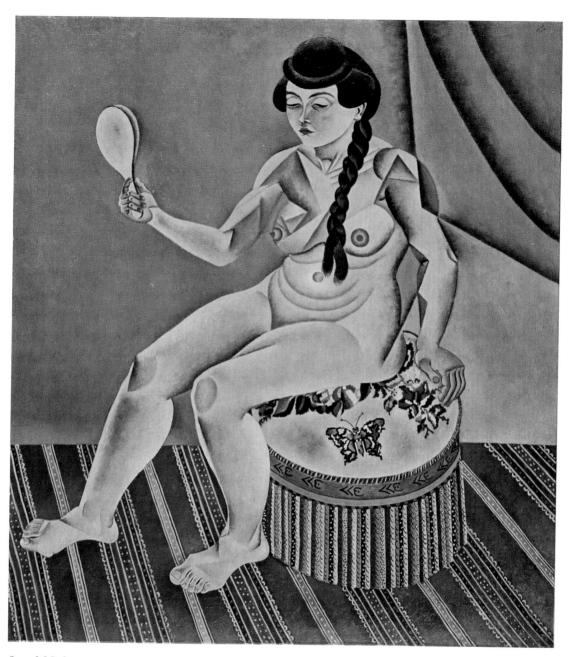

Seated Nude. 1919. Oil on canvas, $44^1/_2 \times 40^1/_8''$. Collection Mr. and Mrs. Pierre Matisse, New York

"Matisse taught us all that autonomous color, with or without modeling, could carry structure through contrasts and subtle juxtapositions." The statement becomes clear if, in relation to some of Miró's own works, one looks at Matisse's *Red Studio* (page 19), with its miraculous firmness of contrapuntal arrangement—bright passages projected against an almost uniform ground. It may be added that Matisse's meaning for Miró is almost precisely the same as for certain painters of today's so called "New York School," who revere the French master's final works which, they say, have opened entirely new ground in the use of color.

Two other notable works of 1919 are *The Olive Grove* (page 23), probably finished before or soon after Miró's arrival in Paris and more assured than his landscapes of the previous year, and the *Self Portrait* (page 26), long a treasured possession of Picasso. The *Self Portrait* is an hypnotic image which anneals convincingly the various influences to which Miró had been exposed in Paris. Apart from its considerable formal virtues, the picture sums up the wide-eyed intentness of the artist's personality, reminding us that Miró has always struck an imponderable balance between inward and outward observation. Its deliberate primitivism recalls a meaningful quotation from the painter himself: "Courage consists in remaining within one's ambience, close to nature, which takes no account of our disasters. Each grain of dust possesses a marvelous soul. But to understand this, it is necessary to rediscover the religious and magic sense of things—that of the primitive peoples."[12]

In 1920 Miró completed a major work of his early career, *The Table* or *Still Life with Rabbit* (opposite). Traces of cubism's influence may be felt in the background, but the objects on the table, among them a live rabbit and rooster, have a new and cohesive strength. The picture has what Georges Hugnet, writing about Miró's art in general, calls "the insolence of candor."[13] Its extreme realism conveys the artist's unabashed delight in his hard-won technical mastery; its color is as vigorous and special as that of the Catalan primitives to whom Miró has so often turned for guidance. The picture was followed in 1921 by the *Portrait of a Spanish Dancer* (page 31). The facial exaggerations in this painting are wonderfully evocative in their roundness; the hard, almost metallic surfaces are strangely warm and alive. Once more it is necessary to stress the psychological astuteness of Miró's portraiture, though its basis is unquestionably poetic rather than intellectual.

The fine *Table with Glove*, also know as *Glove and Newspaper*, of 1921 (page 30) is

Opposite: *The Table (Still Life with Rabbit)*. 1920. Oil on canvas, $51^1/_4 \times 43^1/_4$". Collection Gustav M. Zumsteg, Zurich

Table with Glove (Glove and Newspaper). 1921. Oil on canvas, $46 \times 35^{1}/_{4}''$. The Museum of Modern Art, New York, gift of Armand G. Erpf

Portrait of a Spanish Dancer. 1921. Oil on canvas.
Collection Pablo Picasso, Vauvenargues, France

comparable in handling to the *Portrait of a Spanish Dancer* in that both are glossy and
bland in texture. At this time Miró's interest in realism was still rising, and the painting of the crumpled glove foretells by sixteen years the meticulous technique to
which the painter was to revert in 1937 when he did the *Still Life with Old Shoe* as a
commentary on the Spanish Civil War (page 89). Moreover, the *Table with Glove*
illustrates Miró's attempt to simplify his forms through a deliberate primitivism
which reflects his regard for the Douanier Rousseau, already mentioned in connection
with the *Seated Nude*.

In 1921 Miró returned again to Montroig and there began the culminating work of his early career, *The Farm* (opposite), finished in the fall of 1922. The picture is so complex and stupendous an achievement that it is hard to keep in mind its relatively modest size; it measures only 48 by 55 inches, and yet has the impact of a mural. Since the picture has long been the property of Ernest Hemingway, it seems appropriate to give his eloquent description of it: "No one could look at it and not know it had been painted by a great painter... It has in it all that you feel about Spain when you are there and all that you feel when you are away and cannot go there... No one else has been able to paint these two very opposing things..."[14]

Miró worked on *The Farm* for a total of nine months, in Montroig, in Barcelona, and finally in his studio on the rue Blomet, Paris. Obviously this was an all-out effort to summarize everything he had felt and learned as a painter. And what is extraordinary is that the picture so successfully combines freshness with calculation. Its scintillating color, its lyricism, its affectionate perception–these are qualities which tend to make one forget how precisely planned the composition is. The picture abounds in parallelisms, in those echoed applications of comparable forms to objects of differing identity of which Juan Gris was fond. To give a few conspicuous examples, the round sun's contours are repeated in the foreground box on which a rooster stands. The columns in a newspaper lying on the ground reappear in the tiles to the left of the central tree. The "A" shape of the ladder in the chicken yard recurs in a stool placed directly behind the dog on the winding path which leads toward a woman washing clothes. And so on. Indeed, every inch of the composition has been thought out with that conscientiousness and patience for which Miró is noted among his friends. For Miró is an extremely "correct" man, who often has planned many of his pictures ahead as components of series, who is said to prefer not to paint on Sundays but instead to put on his derby hat and best suit and attend church with his family. Yet there is throughout *The Farm* a marvelous spontaneity, as though the whole image had occurred to the artist in an especially vivid dream, all at once and instantaneously. As to freshness of conception and execution, *The Farm* can stand comparison with the Douanier's famous *Sleeping Gypsy*, so that it is no wonder that Georges Hugnet once called Miró "the purest man since Rousseau."[15]

he Farm. 1921–22. Oil on canvas, 48¹/₄ × 55¹/₄″. Collection Ernest Hemingway, Havana

During the year 1922–23, perhaps as a respite from his strenuous labors on *The Farm*, Miró completed a small group of straightforward and realistic still lifes of which *The Ear of Grain* (below) may be taken as a representative example. One assumes that he decided to sharpen his technique and to restudy commonplace objects to see what could be made of them as part of his painter's vocabulary. But nothing for long could hold in check his growing fantasy of mind. That same year the spirit of *The Farm* was revived in *The Farmer's Wife* (opposite) whose monumental distortions, notably in the handling of the woman's feet, are combined with a new and abstract simplicity;

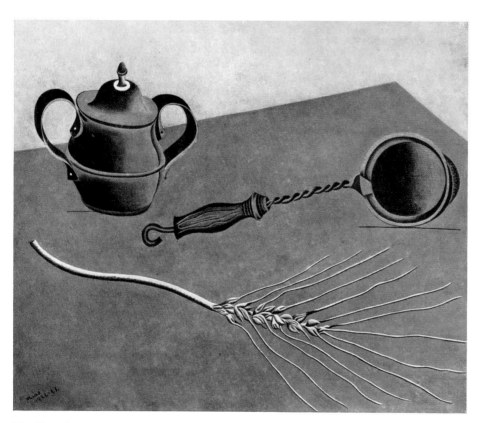

The Ear of Grain. 1922–23. Oil on canvas, $14^7/_8 \times 18^1/_8$″. The Museum of Modern Art, New York. Purchase

34

The Farmer's Wife. 1922–23. Oil on canvas, $31^3/_4 \times 25^1/_2$″. Collection Mrs. Marcel Duchamp, New York

a few large forms predominant. The following year, however, Miró again returned to that inventive profusion of motifs which had characterized *The Farm*. In 1923–24 he painted *The Tilled Field* (opposite) wherein is included the sort of chimerical bestiary which has reminded various critics of Bosch. The picture turns sharply away from the realism of the 1922–23 still lifes and depicts an unlikely but enchanting medley of strange appearances–a human ear attached to a pole, an unbelievably elongated ox drawing a plow, a most capricious horse. The color is varied and insolent, the scenario far transcends whimsy to arrive at comedy of a very high order, like that of the Flemish fantasists but completely Spanish.

Vase of Flowers and Butterfly. 1922–23. Tempera on wood, $32 \times 25^{3}/_{8}''$. Collection **Dr.** and **Mrs.** Leslie M. Maitland, Los Angeles

The Tilled Field. 1923–24. Oil on canvas, 26×37″. Collection Mr. and Mrs. Henry Clifford, Radnor, Pennsylvania

In 1923–24 Miró executed one of the most poetic of his earlier paintings: the *Catalan Landscape*, also known as *The Hunter* (page 39). Whereas the color in *The Tilled Field* had been brazen, now the background is composed of two broad areas of soft, fresco-like yellows and pinks. At first glance one thinks of the picture as an abstraction. Then, remembering Miró's avowed wish to "go beyond form to achieve poetry," one begins to discover a narrative meaning. In Alfred Barr's words, "The picture's subtitle, *The Hunter*, identifies the principal human figure who stands mustached and bearded, a pipe in his mouth, a heart palpitating in his breast; his right hand holds his leashed dog, his left a flaming gun; a trail winds before him. Across the foreground races a rabbit with frightened eye and triangular tail. In the distance is a

37

round tree with a leaf and beyond that the hunter's eye or perhaps the sun, the 'eye of day,' as Shakespeare put it."[16] At the lower right the letters S A R D are an abbreviation of Sardana, the popular Catalan folk dance and at the upper right, presumably on a boat, flies the Spanish naval flag. Thus the painting's iconography is mostly legible after all, even if an understanding of it is by no means essential to an appreciation of Miró's uncanny pictorial eloquence, his piquant arrangement of triangular, rounded, and curlicued forms.

At this stage in his career Miró was much in the company of poets, chiefly of dadaist persuasion. The surrealist movement was about to be launched by André Breton's *Manifeste du Surréalisme, Poisson Soluble*, and by the publication of the important magazine, *La Révolution Surréaliste*, with Pierre Naville, Benjamin Péret and

The Family. (1924). Chalk drawing on glass paper, 29$^1/_2$×41″. The Minneapolis Institute of Arts

Catalan Landscape (The Hunter). 1923–24. Oil on canvas, $25^{1}/_{2} \times 39^{1}/_{2}$". The Museum of Modern Art, New York. Purchase

later Breton as editors. It was an exciting moment in Parisian art and letters, and Miró, whom Breton was soon to call "the most 'surrealist' of us all,"[17] was undoubtedly fascinated by the imaginative liberties which Surrealism proposed. He took an active part in the movement and, as Breton declared, "The tumultuous entrance of Miró in 1924 marks an important step in the development of surrealist art."[18] Miró's new interest in Surrealism is typified by *The Somersault*,[19] which incidentally was the first of his works to be exhibited publicly in America, and *The Family* (opposite). At this time, too, the artist completed a number of large surrealist drawings.

In 1924 Miró painted the sparse, poetic *Maternity* and began the fantastic *Landscape* (pages 40–41). In 1924–25 he also returned to the iconographical complexity of the

Landscape. (1924–25). Oil on canvas. Doucet Foundation, Paris

Opposite: *Maternity*. 1924. Oil on canvas, $36^3/_8 \times 28^3/_4''$. Collection Roland Penrose, London

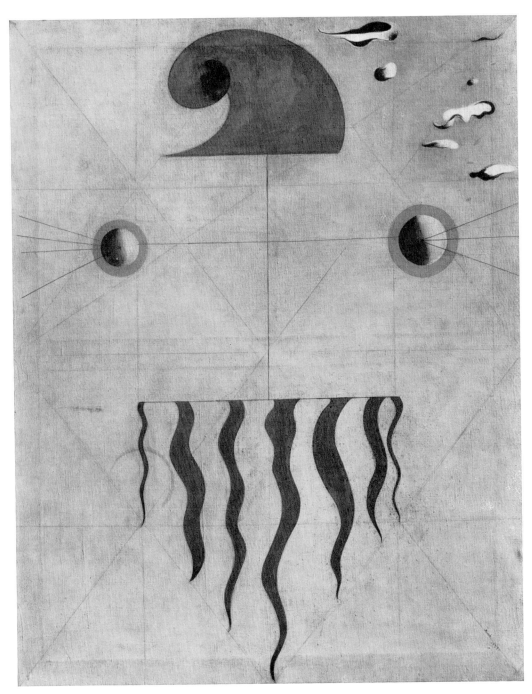

Catalan Peasant. (1924–25). Oil on canvas. Collection Roland Penrose, London

Head of a Peasant. 1924–25. Oil on canvas, $18^{1}/_{2} \times 17^{1}/_{2}''$. Private collection, Paris

The Harlequin's Carnival. 1924–25. Oil on canvas, $25^1/_4 \times 35^7/_8''$. Room of Contemporary Art, Albright Art Gallery, Buffalo

Catalan Landscape in *The Harlequin's Carnival* (opposite). At the left appears a ladder ("Another recurrent form in my work is the ladder," Miró himself has said)[20] with the ubiquitous ear attached. The background of the composition is bisected in the manner he had admired in Urgell's paintings, and against the flooring and the wall a riotous carnival takes place, with chimerical beasties and enigmatic objects placed about in amiable profusion. On the wall there hangs a draftsman's triangle, an object Miró may have come to admire in Giorgio de Chirico's metaphysical works, and beside it an open window extends the picture space. The playful spirit of the painting is abetted by brilliant colors—reds, blues, greens, whites, and yellows; the puppet-like character of the figures recalls the fact that Alfred Jarry, whose famous *Ubu Roi* was written for puppets, was at that time one of Miró's preferred authors. The one human protagonist in the carnival is the bearded man with pipe, an image to which Miró has returned often, as various critics have pointed out.

1925–27

Up to this point in his career, Miró had been greatly concerned with subject matter, however obliquely and regardless of strong overtones of fantasy. From the early landscapes and portraits up through *The Farm* and on to *The Tilled Field* and *Harlequin's Carnival*, he had painted more or less objectively, each picture depicting a separate imagery, whether based on actual experience and tangible appearances or proceeding directly from hallucination and dreams. In 1928, as we shall see, he was to return to this sort of representation in the fine series of so-called "Dutch Interiors," inspired by his trip to Holland. But meanwhile he completed a group of far more abstract pictures, as though he had taken to heart Breton's definition of Surrealism as "thought's dictation, all exercise of reason and every esthetic or moral pre-occupation being absent."[21] It remains to be said that Breton's definition begins with the words "pure psychic automatism,"[22] and that many of Miró's colleagues were now experimenting avidly with automatic painting, that is, painting in which recognizable objects and figures rarely appeared. This more abstract direction in surrealist art attracted some of the movement's most talented adherents for a time, though it never wholly obscured the carefully defined irrationality of men like de Chirico, first of all, and afterwards Tanguy, Dali, Magritte, and Delvaux, among others.

At any rate during the mid-1920s Miró painted a superb series of freely organized and relatively abstract works. Among them are the *Man with a Pipe* (page 50), *The*

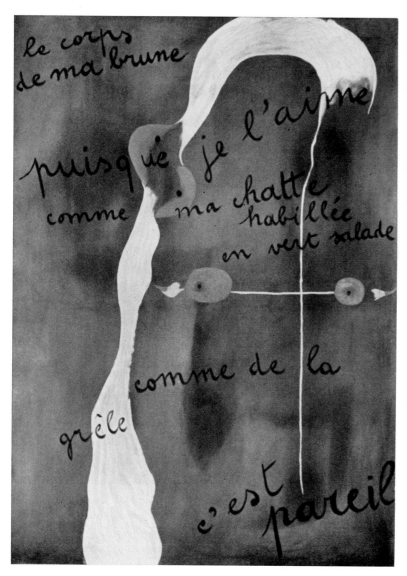

"Le corps de ma brune . . ." 1925. Oil on canvas, $51\frac{1}{8} \times 38\frac{1}{4}$".
Collection Mme Marie Cuttoli, Paris

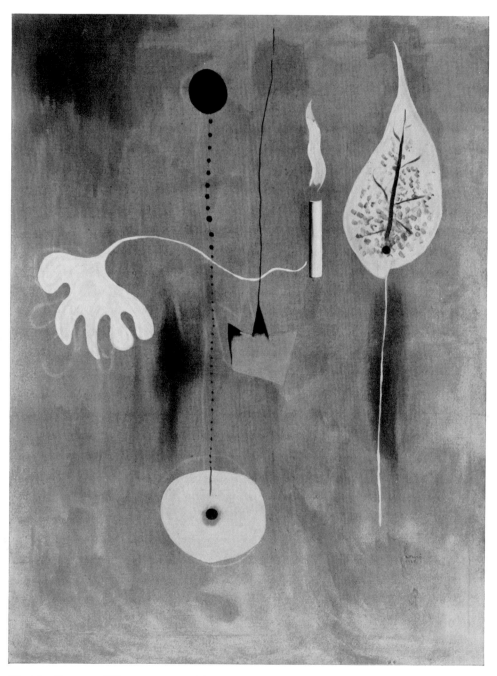

The Candle. 1925. Oil on canvas, 45⁷/₈×35″. Collection Mr. and Mrs. Paul Lester Wiener, New York

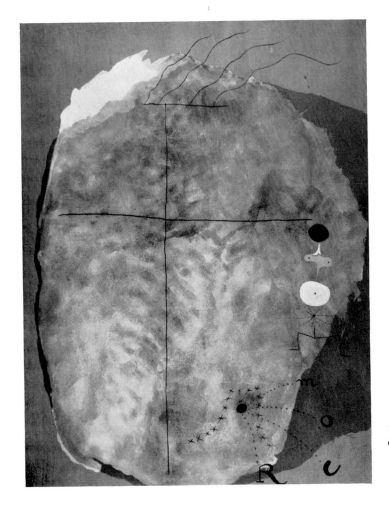

Candle (page 47), so deliciously luminous and poetic in surface, *Painting* (opposite), with its wavy *café-au-lait* background, and *"Le corps de ma brune..."* (page 46), one of the very finest of those pictures in which Miró made liberal use of written words as an integral element of his plastic order and at the same time as an affirmation of his profound interest in poetry for its own sake.

1925 was a vintage year for such abstractions which are sometimes painted on a soft brown ground and again on blue, "a savage blue, insolent, electric, which sufficed by itself to make the canvas vibrate," as René Gaffé, one of Miró's first champions, put the matter.[23] But in 1926 and 1927 Miró's interest in more readable fantasy revived

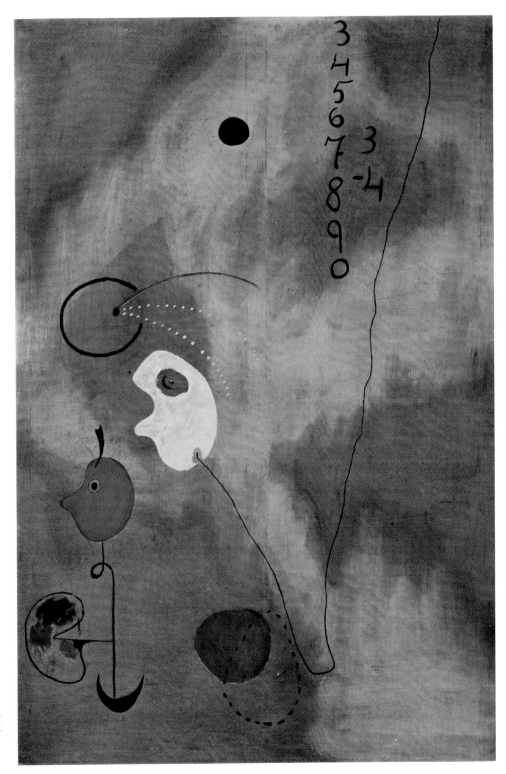

Painting. 1925. Oil on canvas,
76⅝ × 51″. Collection Mr. and
Mrs. Pierre Matisse, New York

Man with a Pipe. 1925. Oil on canvas, 57³/₈ × 45″. Private collection, New York

Fratellini. 1927. Oil on canvas, $51^{1}/_{4} \times 38''$. Collection Mr. and Mrs. Harry Lewis, Winston, Birmingham, Michigan

Nude. 1926. Oil on canvas, $36^1/_4 \times 29^5/_8''$. The Louise and Walter Arensberg Collection, Philadelphia Museum of Art

in the admirable *Nude*, the *Dog Barking at the Moon*, for a long time perhaps the best known of his paintings in this country, and the *Fratellini*, an immensely appealing image of the celebrated family of circus clowns (pages 51–53). At this point Miró seemingly could do no wrong, and first-rate paintings followed one another in splendid profusion.

By now Miró had at last won recognition; his second one-man show in Paris was attended and admired by a number of the most influential and talented men in the French capital's professional world of art and letters. He had also begun to sell, though still at modest prices. In 1928 he was able to afford a trip to Holland and thus break the pattern of a life heretofore entirely spent in Catalonia or Paris.

Dog Barking at the Moon. 1926. Oil on canvas, 28³/₄ × 36¹/₄". A. E. Gallatin Collection, Philadelphia Museum of Art

Dutch Interior. (1928). Oil on canvas, 28¹/₂ × 35¹/₂″. Collection Miss Peggy Guggenheim, Venice

Jan Steen (1626–1679): *The Cat's Dancing Lesson.*
Oil on wood, 25^1/$_2$×23^1/$_4$". Rijksmuseum, Amsterdam

1928: THE DUTCH INTERIORS

In Holland Miró was enthralled by the works of the Dutch Little Masters of the seventeenth century as he saw them in various museums, notably Amsterdam's Rijksmuseum. We know from James Sweeney's account, based on information from the artist himself, that the painter bought in Holland and took home to Paris a number of postcards of these Dutch pictures, among them one of Jan Steen's *The Cat's Dancing Lesson* (above), which became the direct source of inspiration for one of his own paintings of 1928 (opposite) in the series known as the Dutch Interiors. As Sweeney points out, Miró has transposed from the Steen "such elements as the guitar, dog, and man's face looking in through an open window."[24] To which may be added that Miró has also transposed in personalized terms the laughing face of the figure at the left of Steen's composition, the contours of the woman playing a musical instrument to the cat and even an abstracted equivalent of her shoe, just above the dog. He has also included the pitcher on a white cloth at the right in

55

Dutch Interior. (1928). Oil on canvas, 50³/₄ × 38″. Collection Mr. and Mrs. Samuel A. Marx, Chicago

Dutch Interior. 1928. Oil on canvas, $36^1/_8 \times 28^3/_4$". The Museum of Modern Art, New York, Mrs. Simon Guggenheim Fund

Steen's work. But all these transpositions are consummately original and can bear comparison with those Picasso has made from various pictures of earlier centuries. Indeed, the two Spaniards have shown an unrivaled talent for this sort of metaphysical conceit in commenting on the art of the past. Miró's picture is altogether memorable in its wit and its bright charm of color.

Two other pictures in the series inspired by Miró's trip to Holland are another *Dutch Interior* (page 56) and the canvas whose cryptic title is *The Potato* (opposite). In both pictures the distortions are overwhelmingly free and imaginative; both have a rhythmic vitality which innumerable other artists, both older and younger than Miró, have admired. Indeed, this is as good a place as any to note that Miró has long been studied with care by painters of advanced inclination here and abroad. His exhibitions are almost invariably crowded with artists (the writer still remembers with a certain awe the excited arrival of Picasso at the opening of one of Miró's Paris shows in the 1930s); he deserves to the utmost that meaningful epithet, "a painters' painter." And if the iconography of *The Potato* is a matter for conjecture only, nothing can obviate its vividness and joyousness as an image. Its spirit seems thoroughly Catalan, its fantasy has deep roots in the long native tradition which extends from the primitive muralists of the Barcelona area to the effulgent *art nouveau* of Antoni Gaudí.

The climax of the Dutch Interior series of 1928 is reached in the Museum of Modern Art's canvas (page 57). For this particular work no single, specific precedent in seventeenth-century Dutch genre painting is known, and it seems probable that it is based on various pictures Miró saw on his trip to Holland and of which he brought back postcards. This in fact was what the painter himself said had been the case in his interview with Edouard Roditi in 1958,[25] though one is obliged to quarrel with Roditi's theory that Miró's Dutch Interiors were derisively intended; they are on the contrary respectful, almost reverent. In the Museum's admirable canvas, animals and musical instruments are placed in the interior with profusion, and there results an atmosphere of giddy wit, reinforced by the gaiety of the colors. It is a picture which provokes laughter, as many of its Dutch prototypes were intended to do, and also respect for the technical facility of its handling. Miró was by now very positive of his gifts, though he had preserved the naivete and playfulness which strengthen rather than weaken the force of his images. The color is so fresh and convincing that it justifies Clement Greenberg's assertion: "Every painter knows how difficult it is to compose in flat colors without employing modulations of dark and

The Potato. (1928). Oil on burlap, $39^5/_8 \times 32^1/_8''$. Private collection, New York

light or a single over-all tone to unify the surface; Miró, along with Matisse and Mondrian, belongs among the few artists in Western tradition who have done this with consistent success."[26]

1929–32

Perhaps as a relief from the tight and cohesive planning of the Dutch Interiors, Miró produced in 1928 and 1929 a number of striking collages, whose deliberate infantilism has the metaphysical intensity of Paul Klee's works. Miró had been introduced to Klee's art in the mid-1920s by his surrealist colleagues, notably Louis Aragon, Paul Eluard and René Crevel (all of whom were writing in praise of the Swiss master at that time), though not André Breton, who failed to reproduce a single Klee painting in his *Le surréalisme et la peinture* of 1928, probably because Klee had no official connection with the surrealist movement of which Breton was the ringmaster. It seems likely that Miró's painter's eye was able to appreciate fully the revolutionary importance of Klee's vision. At any rate, there is a certain affinity between some of Miró's more casual works of 1929 and Klee's magic watercolors and drawings. Both artists have been responsible for an incalculable extension of humor's capacity to be expressed in purely visual terms.

In 1929 Miró's most ambitious if short series of paintings consisted of "imaginary" portraits of female figures from the past, including *"La Fornarina"* and *Portrait of Mrs. Mills in 1750* (pages 63 and 65). The first of these two paintings was based on a postcard or other reproduction of Raphael's picture by the same name in the Barberini Palace in Rome (page 150), and Miró has transposed the sweeping, rounded contours of the bare shoulders of Raphael's model and the V shape of the garment she holds between her breasts. Moreover, it seems possible that the dark spot on the curious white form near the top of Miró's image is derived in reverse color from the pearl La Fornarina wears in her hair. As to the *Portrait of Mrs. Mills in 1750* there has long been a theory that its inspiration was a portrait by Gainsborough or Constable. But a careful search through documents on the art of these two English masters has revealed no painting of a Mrs. Mills. We do, however, know of a *Portrait of Mrs. Mills* (page 62), by George Engleheart, a pupil of Sir Joshua Reynolds. The interrelationship between Miró's image and Engleheart's is striking. In both paintings the figure wears a large hat; in both she holds out a white sheaf of paper which in the Engleheart is a letter and in the Miró either that or a sheet of music. (In actual life Mrs. Mills

Spanish Dancer. 1928. Paper, string, metal, 42 × 26³/₄″. Collection Mr. and Mrs. Morton G. Neumann, Chicago

George Engleheart (1752–1829): *Portrait of Mrs. Mills* (after an engraving by J. R. Smith)

was a singer.) The Engleheart portrait had been engraved by one John R. Smith, and a copy of the engraving may well have come into Miró's hands.*

Precisely why Miró should have been beguiled by such figures from the art of the past is not a matter of clear record, despite questioning of the artist himself by several friends and critics, among them the writer. It seems possible that he had become interested in the curvilinear forms of earlier epochs' figures and costumes and that these forms confirmed his perennial regard for the sweeping arabesques which reached a late climax in the *art nouveau* style. Moreover, the biomorphic character of the contours in Miró's 1929 "portraits" suggests some influence from his good friend–and in 1925-26 his close neighbor– Jean (Hans) Arp, who had already invented a whole new vocabulary of living as opposed to geometric shapes, based on leaves, clouds, the

* Since the above was written Miró has confirmed the fact that Engleheart's picture was indeed the one he took as point of departure for his *Mrs. Mills in 1750*. He adds that not until now had he known the identity of the painter of the British portrait.

Portrait of Mrs. Mills in 1750. 1929. Oil on canvas, $45^1/_2 \times 35''$. Private collection, New Canaan, Connecticut

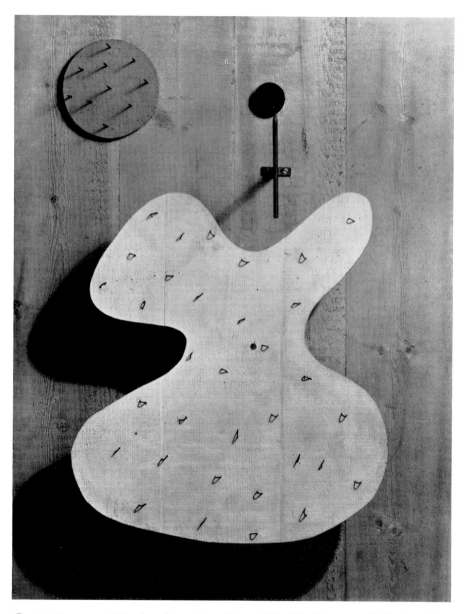

Construction. 1930. Wood and metal, $35\,^{7}/_{8} \times 27\,^{5}/_{8}''$. The Museum of Modern Art, New York. Purchase

"La Fornarina." 1929. Oil on burlap, $57^1/_2 \times 45''$. Collection Robert J. Schoelkopf, Jr., New York

human torso, etc. More specifically, Miró's "portraits" recall Arp's *Madame Torso with Wavy Hat* of 1916 (page 150), though the latter artist has denied vehemently that he ever influenced his younger friend, insisting that Miró arrived at his style by quite another route – the art of children and the early Catalan frescoes. In any case, the most impressive picture in the 1929 series is the *Portrait of Mrs. Mills in 1750*, with its rich chocolate browns, reds, yellows, greens, purples, and blacks, its beautifully soft texture which was indeed, as Miró has told the writer, inspired by Catalan wall paintings.

In the early 1930s, Miró appears to have painted a number of large and quickly executed pictures, outstanding among them being the *Man, Woman, and Child* of the latter year (opposite). From these years too date some of his finest relief constructions (page 64), in which with metal and wood he achieved a personal extension of his aims as a painter. He also completed the ferociously active *Composition* (page 68) whose frenzied forms swirl upward against a partially backlit ground (the picture, alas, was destroyed during the recent war). At this time, as Christian Zervos has remarked, "Miró no longer prepares his paintings; he gives them not the slightest thought in the world before taking brush or pencil in hand. He departs from nothingness with the point of view of conscious effort, but this is a nothingness rich in all the dreams of a true poet. The forms install themselves on the canvas without a preconceived idea. He begins them by spilling a little color on the surface and then circulates a dipped brush around the canvas. As his hand moves, the obscure vision becomes precise."[27]

If Miró worked in a more or less automatic fashion during much of this period, in 1932 he executed a group of small pictures on wooden panels whose precision can hardly have been the result of so casual a technique. One of the most vivid of these is the little *Seated Woman* (page 69), with its enameled surface and brilliant color. It seems a pity that Miró did not produce more works in this estimable vein, but much of his time was now spent designing the scenery and costumes for Léonide Massine's ballet, *Jeux d'Enfants* (page 71), a project with which he busied himself through the spring of 1932. This was the second time he had undertaken theatrical design; in 1925 he had collaborated with Max Ernst in creating the sets and costumes for Diaghilev's ballet, *Roméo et Juliette*. One senses, however, that like his countryman, Juan Gris, Miró was made rather uneasy by the demands of the theatre though he had avidly attended the ballet as a youth in Spain.[28] Essentially unworldly in temperament, he probably found it difficult to adjust to the theatre's very real need for artifice, though it must be admitted that judging by existing sketches and photographs his work for *Jeux d'Enfants* is far from negligible.

Man, Woman, and Child. February 1931. Oil on canvas, 35 × 45 ⁵/₈″. The Louise and Walter Arensberg Collection, Philadelphia Museum of Art

Composition. (1932). Formerly collection Theodor Werner, Berlin (now destroyed)

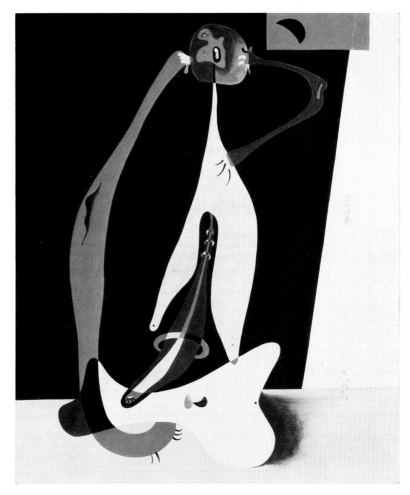

Seated Woman. October 1932. Oil on wood, $18^{1}/_{4} \times 15''$. Private collection, New York

It is difficult to make precise what effect Miró's work for the theatre had on his easel painting. It seems reasonable to suppose, nevertheless, that his experience in making maquettes and drawings for stage purposes encouraged him to adopt a new if temporary system as a painter. In Barcelona in the winter of 1933 he began to paste on the walls of his studio scraps of paper to form a more or less continuous collage from which he drew the ideas for pictures, adopting one paper form here, another there, as the spirit moved him. In his words, "In 1933 . . . I used to tear newspapers into rough shapes and paste them on cardboards. Day after day I would accumulate such shapes. After the collages were finished they served me as points of departure for paintings. I did not copy the collages. I merely let them suggest shapes to me..."[29] His experiments paved the way for one of the outstanding series of paintings of his entire career—the large, abstract compositions of 1933.

1933–34: PAINTINGS, COLLAGES, PASTELS

The 1933 paintings are so even in quality that it is hard to decide which among them is the most impressive. One of the largest is the Museum of Modern Art's *Painting* (page 73) for which the preliminary collage still exists (page 149) and which Alfred Barr has described as follows: "Against a softly atmospheric background are suspended, silhouetted or outlined forms which suggest a pastoral with a seated dog and horned cattle. The composition is remarkable in Miró's art for its serenity and elegance."[30] We know now from the evidence of the collage on which the picture was based that the horned shapes were in fact derived from the armatures of machinery. Nevertheless, Miró was entirely capable of giving such mechanical objects an animistic significance. The supposition that he did so is reinforced by the Wadsworth Atheneum's picture (page 72) from the same series, wherein some of the forms are more decipherable and specifically animal-like. In both pictures there are few accents of bright color and the principal elements are painted in that rich black which Miró has often used to marvelous effect. The drawing is firm and assured; the transitions of tone in the background exceptionally subtle. Seldom in his long and distinguished career has Miró surpassed these and other paintings of 1933 for impetus of creative abandon.

Perhaps as respite from the large abstractions, Miró at this time created some of his wittiest collages, combining drawing with postcards, pasted-on engravings, photographs and odds and ends of such materials as string, felt, and metal (pages 74 and 75). In some of these he draws close to Max Ernst, though the forms are entirely his own

Sketch for Léonide Massine's ballet *"Jeux
d'Enfants."* March 1932. Gouache, 19¹/₈×25".
Collection Gérald Cramer, Geneva

Léonide Massine's ballet *"Jeux d'Enfants."*
1932. Decor by Miró

Painting. June 10, 1933. Oil on canvas, $51^1/_4 \times 63^1/_2''$. Wadsworth Atheneum, Hartford, Ella Gallup Sumner and Mary Catlin Sumner Collection

ainting. June 13, 1933. Oil on canvas, $68^1/_2 \times 77^1/_4''$. The Museum of Modern Art, New York, gift of the Advisory Committee

and the humor more playful and naive than it is in the collages of his sophisticated German contemporary. Miró's interest in texture was becoming steadily more pronounced, and he now often painted on sandpaper and other rough surfaces. In 1934 he also began a series of pastels (pages 78 and 79) some of which, it must be admitted, are rather scatologic. Miró has made frequent use of genitals as symbols in his art. Yet his attitude toward sex is fundamentally innocent and far from vicious. It proceeds from a childlike curiosity and glee; it is unashamed and frank rather than salacious.

One of the most ambitious and successful paintings Miró executed in 1934 is "L'hirondelle d'amour" (page 81) done as a cartoon for a tapestry. *Hirondelle* means swallow, and the picture's swooping, darting forms do indeed suggest a swallow's flight, though some of its birdlike forms have human heads. This is also an image of ecstasy, described in colors which are unusually exhilarated and bold even for Miró, who has always been fearless in matters of tonal invention. What irrepressible gaiety this bacchanal of the sky conveys! In terms of headlong flourish it is assuredly among the most remarkable of Miró's paintings of the mid-1930s.

In the *Person in the Presence of Nature* of 1935 (page 83) Miró again displays his

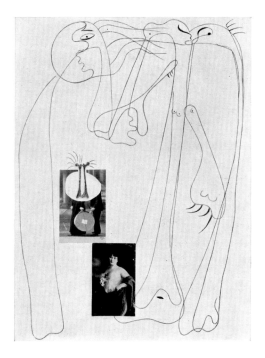

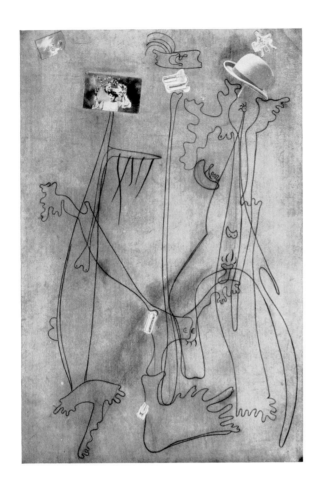 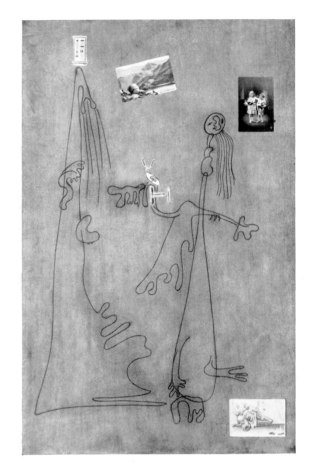

Above left: *Collage*. September 25, 1933. Charcoal and pasted papers, 42 × 27¹/₂″. Collection Mr. and Mrs. Morton G. Neumann, Chicago

Above right: *Collage*. September 8, 1933. Charcoal and pasted papers, 42 × 28″. Pierre Matisse Gallery, New York

Opposite left: *Collage*. September 4, 1933. Crayon and pasted papers, 24¹/₂ × 18¹/₂″. Private collection, New York

Opposite right: *Collage ("Le Papillon")*. (1933). Pasted paper, butterfly wing, charcoal and watercolor, 25 × 18³/₄″. Collection Mr. and Mrs. B. H. Friedman, New York

Rope and People. 1935. Oil on cardboard with coil of rope, $41^1/_4 \times 29^3/_8''$. The Museum of Modern Art, New York, given anonymously

"Objet." (1931). Painted wood with feather and metals, 44⁷/₈ × 28³/₄". Collection Mr. and Mrs. William N. Copley, Longpoint-sur-Orage, France

Left: *"Objet poétique."* (1936). Wood, man's hat, and stuffed parrot, 33¹/₄" high. Collection Mr. and Mrs. Pierre Matisse, New York

Woman. (1934). Pastel, 42⁷/₈ × 28³/₄″. Galerie Maeght, Paris

Opposite: *Figure.* October 1934. Pastel, 41³/₄ × 27⁷/₈″. Collection Mrs. A. Conger Goodyear, New York

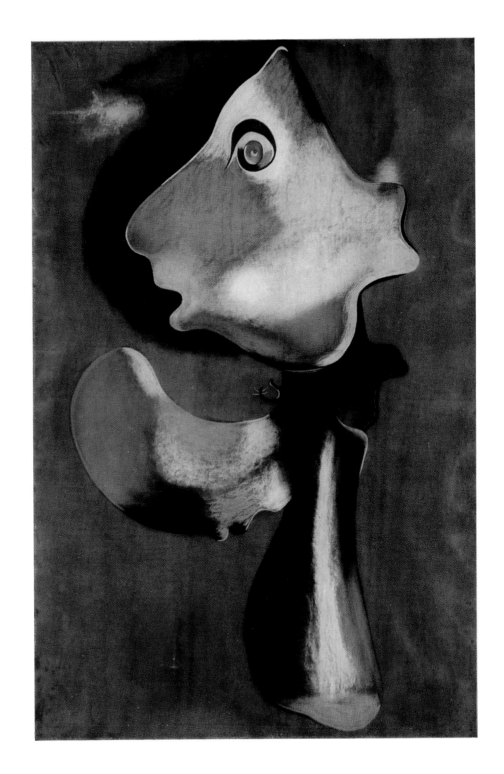

perennial interest in creating bestiaries. Here once more his art suggests parallels with the Flemish painters of fantasy, notably in the conception of the long-nosed creature at the right. But his quality remains Spanish and his humor, even when ferocious as in the figure against the sky, is nevertheless also playful and childlike. This humor, however, turns quite malignant in the *Head of a Man* (page 82), surely one of the most savage works of Miró's career, modeled with uncanny firmness and skill, so that its effect is sculptural.

Related in iconography to the *Person in the Presence of Nature* are two small but exceptionally colorful paintings, the *Persons Attracted by the Form of the Mountain* and the *Figures and Mountains* (pages 85 and 86). These two pictures are a very long cry indeed from the realistic landscapes of Miró's early career, not only in their inclusion of monstrously fantastic figures, but in the way the terrain is abstracted into unlikely plains and knolls, painted in glaring reds, greens, yellows, and blues. The animals are like the beasties of dreams or the imaginings of a gifted child. Yet one must not overlook the discipline which underlies their subtle plastic relationships one to another, their strange believeability which transcends whimsy by far. Miró's mood seems to have been especially joyful at this moment, as when he made the poetic construction with parrot (page 77). It was to darken as the growing fury of the Spanish Civil War (July, 1936–March, 1939) cut him off from Montroig and Barcelona and aroused his sympathy for the suffering of his people.

1937: THE WAR IN SPAIN

Among his friends Miró is known for his almost total lack of interest in political matters. At the same time, he cannot have failed to have been outraged by the atrocities of General Franco's Fascist and Nazi allies. Moreover, it is no exaggeration to say that the Spanish Civil War stirred the artists and writers of Europe (and America) as they had not been stirred by a foreign issue since the Greek War of Independence, when men as different in temperament as Byron and Delacroix were impelled to protest. At any rate, in 1937 Miró, perhaps as a deliberate foil to Picasso's magnificent *Guernica*, produced a work unique in his career as an easel painter: the *Still Life with Old Shoe* (page 89), a tragic and forceful summary of his emotions about the war.

Pierre Loeb, at that time Miró's Paris dealer, has said that the artist set up on a table on the second floor of Loeb's gallery on the rue des Beaux-Arts an actual still life consisting of an apple[31] pierced by tines, a gin bottle with paper wrapping, a loaf

"L'hirondelle d'amour." (1934). Oil on canvas, $78^1/_2 \times 97^1/_2$". Collection Nelson A. Rockefeller, New York

Head of a Man. (1935). Oil on cardboard, $41^1/_2 \times 29^3/_8''$. Private collection, New York

of bread, and an old shoe, and painted it all of every day for a month. (Afterwards Miró took the picture back to his new studio on the rue Blanqui to finish; it is dated on the back January 24–May 29, 1937.) For the melancholy protest Miró wished to make against Spain's poverty and suffering, a return to the realism of his early career must have seemed necessary. The colors are dark and lurid. In the sky a poltergeist-like shadow floats in from the left, the bottle casts a heavy shadow and ominous black clouds fill the upper right section. The apple is savagely impaled by the fork, the loaf of bread's carved end becomes a skull, and even the gin bottle with its grimacing

Person in the Presence of Nature. (1935). Gouache on cardboard, 29³/₄ × 41¹/₂″. The Louise and Walter Arensberg Collection, Philadelphia Museum of Art

Nocturne. November 9 – 16, 1935. Oil on copper, $16^7/_8 \times 11^3/_4''$. Collection
Roland Penrose, London

Persons Attracted by the Form of the Mountain. (1936?). Tempera on masonite, $12^3/_4 \times 19^1/_2''$. The Baltimore Museum of Art, Saidie A. May Collection

Two Personages in Love with a Woman. May 1936. Oil on copper, $10 \times 14''$. Pierre Matisse Gallery, New York

Figures and Mountains. May 1936.
Tempera on masonite, $11^7/_8 \times 9^7/_8''$.
Collection Mr. and Mrs. Lee A. Ault,
New York

letters, G I, seems menaced by the upheld, ragged ends of its own wrapping. The more gentle colors of the old shoe do nothing to obviate its vitality as a symbol of need; the callouses and wrinkles of long wear are effectively defined, and one senses the weariness of the foot it once encased.

To create so memorable a polemic work of art in terms of still life is a very considerable achievement, not unworthy of its allegorical companion piece, Picasso's *Guernica*. It remains to be said, however, that the picture seemed to some of Miró's more abstract-minded champions a betrayal of his innate gifts. The Surrealists, on the other hand, and indeed many of those admirers of the artist who are not disturbed by hu-

Persons in the Presence of a Metamorphosis. January 1936. Tempera on masonite, $19^{1}/_{2} \times 22^{3}/_{8}''$. Private collection, New York   *New Orleans Museum of Art*

manistic or psychological content, have praised the image enthusiastically. For quite apart from its subject matter, the picture is beautifully composed and its captivating fluidity of tone repays our closest scrutiny. Miró himself is justifiably proud of this painting. Some years ago he told the writer that it foretold a direction he would like to follow more and more often as a gesture of protest against the decorative tendencies of much abstract art he saw around him. There is no evidence that he has done so on an easel scale. Perhaps only the horrors of war in his beloved Spain could have prompted him to paint this unique and haunting picture.

For the stairwell of the Spanish Pavilion at the Paris Exposition of 1937 Miró created a large mural on masonite panels entitled *The Reaper* (page 90). It has sometimes been assumed that in painting the mural Miró turned his back on the politico-sociological commentary which is so unmistakable in the *Still Life with Old Shoe.* Indeed, James Sweeney, Miró's persuasive champion for many years, has declared that in the mural "we see a return to the more fantastic decorative spirit which had characterized his earlier work as a whole."[32] But to the writer, who saw the mural at the Exposition on many occasions, it has always seemed more than possible that its ferocious and tormented central figure of a reaper with sickle was intended to have a symbolic as opposed to a decorative meaning, especially since Picasso's thoroughly anti-ornamental *Guernica* was hanging in the same building.

Two theories as to the significance of the mural's iconography have been advanced. Juan Larrea has suggested a possible derivation from a passage in the Apocalypse (Revelation XIV, 17–20) in which a reaper with sickle gathered grapevines and cast them into "the great winepress of the wrath of God," whence they flowed forth as blood "even unto the horse bridles, by the space of a thousand and six hundred furlongs."[33]

A symbolic reference to the devastation of war seems obvious here. But Larrea, a friend of Miró, also mentions the more likely possibility that the artist had been inspired in his choice of subject by the national Catalan song of liberation whose title is *"Els Segadors,"* meaning the reapers. This theory has been confirmed in conversation with José Luis Sert, who as co-architect for the Spanish Pavilion was naturally in close touch with Miró while the mural was being executed. Moreover, Miró's anti-

Pablo Picasso: *Guernica.* (1937).
Oil on canvas, $11'5\frac{1}{2}'' \times 25'5\frac{3}{4}''$.
Extended loan by the artist to
Museum of Modern Art, New York

88

Still Life with Old Shoe. January 24 – May 29, 1937. Oil on canvas, $32^1/_4 \times 46''$. Private collection, New Canaan, Connecticut

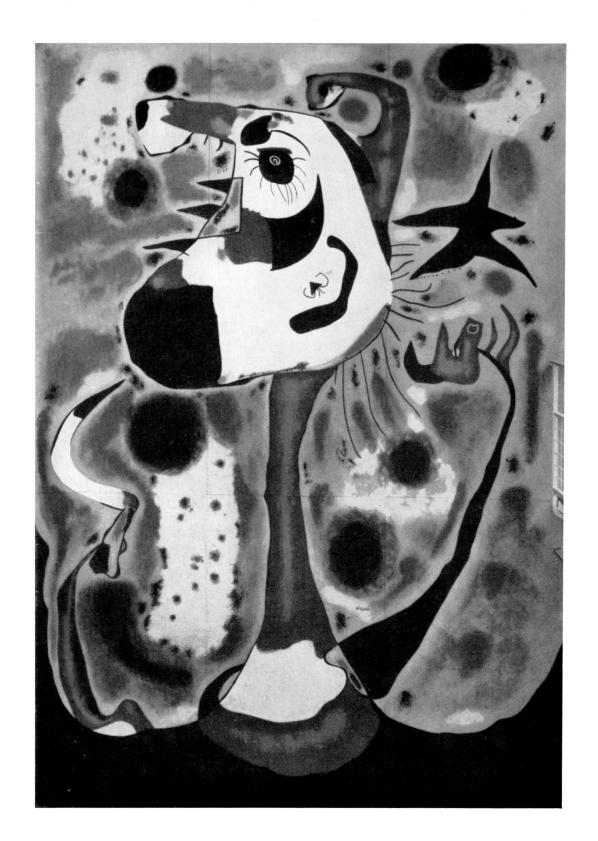

Franco poster, *Help Spain* (below), executed at this same time treats a comparable subject. The inscription on the poster as translated from the French by Peter Watson reads: "In the present struggle I see, on the Fascist side, spent forces; on the opposite side, the people, whose boundless creative will gives Spain an impetus which will astonish the world."[34]

After the Paris Exposition closed, Miró's mural was sent to Valencia, where its masonite panels were soon lost and possibly destroyed. The loss is serious, since no one who saw the mural in place in the Spanish Pavilion is likely to forget its strong and poignant efficacy as a symbol of oppression. Nor does one forget the mastery with which Miró covered the huge stairwell of the pavilion, though presumably he had never worked on so large a scale before. Since that time, in a more decorative vein, the painter has completed several murals in oil (pages 98, 122 and 130). They hold their huge spaces with abundant ease.

Opposite: *The Reaper*. Mural decoration for Paris Exposition (1937). Oil on masonite, 13'6" × 8'2$\frac{1}{2}$" (present whereabouts unknown).

Help Spain (Aidez Espagne). (1937). Color stencil, 9$\frac{3}{4}$ × 7$\frac{5}{8}$". The Museum of Modern Art, New York, gift of Pierre Matisse

Self Portrait. 1937–38. Pencil, crayon and oil on canvas, $57^{1}/_{2} \times 38^{1}/_{4}''$. Private collection, New Canaan, Connecticut

In 1937-38, Miró executed a masterful self portrait (opposite), in which color is reduced to minor accents and the drawing is hypnotically intense and skilled. The image is at once a triumph of self-examination and a technical *tour de force* of the finest order. It is also a virtual anthology of those cryptic forms – stars, pinwheels, and inexplicable objects – of which the artist has always been fond. There is a theory, unconfirmed by Miró himself in writing, that the picture represents the painter's conception of himself ascending to heaven, and indeed there is an uprising and celestial atmosphere about the picture which defies precise analysis but is strongly felt by most observers. The staring pinwheel eyes dominate the head; the fluted stylizations of the nose, upper lip, and chin are original and sensitive. And throughout the image are embedded appealing baubles in the shape of sunbursts and starfish, like useless but treasured objects on a nursery shelf. This beyond question is one of the major portraits of our time.

Certain critics have wondered why Miró, so superb a colorist, used so little color in the *Self Portrait*. (Significantly, it was at this time that the artist first became engrossed in making etchings and aquatints, and their calligraphy almost certainly had some effect on his linear preoccupations in the *Self Portrait*.) The fact is that he tried his hand at another version of the picture in color. According to an eye witness, Pierre Matisse, the original version was done in a small room in Miró's apartment on the rue Blanqui. On one side of the room Miró had hung a round, convex mirror whose magnification undoubtedly affected the artist's drawing and accounts at least in part for the image's looming monumentality, its glacial aggrandizements. On the other side of the room Miró placed his easel, and during the entire time the picture was being painted turned back and forth from mirror to canvas. When the portrait was completed he decided to try his hand at a second and much more colorful version. He therefore traced the composition on another canvas of the same size and pondered the problem of strengthening the tonal brilliance. He quickly came to the conclusion that the original version was complete in itself, and the tracing was abandoned, though a photograph of it has survived and been published.[35] Moreover, the portrait was converted into an etching, in 1938, by Miró in collaboration with Louis Marcoussis.

Portraiture must have been much on Miró's mind during the troubled year before World War II broke out, since in 1938 he finished a short series of figure pieces

Portrait IV. (1938). Oil on canvas, 51¹/₄ × 38¹/₄″. Collection Mr. and Mrs. G. David Thompson, Pittsburgh

Opposite: *Portrait I.* 1938. Oil on canvas, 63³/₄ × 51¹/₄″. The Baltimore Museum of Art, Saidie A. May Collection

which he called portraits, though clearly they resemble no actual persons. The finest works in the series are the *Portrait I*, with butterfly mouth and a star and sunburst for eyes, and the *Portrait IV*, whose whirligig structure puts one in mind of a Calder mobile (pages 94 and 95). After the linear discipline of the *Self Portrait* the painter returned in these two pictures to the forceful colors he had used with such assurance for many years.

In 1938, too, Miró completed the fine *Nocturne* (below) and the *Painting-poem* (opposite). In the latter image written words play a predominant role and remind us of the painter's own words: "I make no distinction between painting and poetry. It

Nocturne. 1938. Oil on masonite, 22 × 29″. Private collection, New York

96

Painting-poem. April 1938. Oil on canvas, 51 × 76⁷/₈″. Pierre Matisse Gallery, New York

Nursery Decoration. September 1938. Oil on canvas, 31⅝" × 10'4". Collection Mr. and Mrs. Richard K. Weil, St. Louis

therefore happens that I illustrate my canvases with poetic phrases and vice versa."[36] It is an estimable achievement that Miró was able to rely so heavily on calligraphy and yet not surrender pictorial impact. We are a long way here from the cubists, who used printed words as mostly subsidiary elements to enliven rather than dominate their compositions.

At some point in 1938 Miró's mood must have turned rather sombre, as when he painted the little *Head of a Woman* (page 101). The woman's head is converted into a monstrous visage; her arms are upflung like the claws of a crab; the color is dark but extremely luminous. Comparable in tonality is the nursery decoration (above) Miró painted for the three children of Pierre Matisse. Considering the purpose for which this panel was executed, it seems rather odd at first glance that its subject

matter should be so distraught and menacing. Yet however malevolent the fanged animal at the right, the picture has an underlying gaiety and cohesive power which make it one of the most admirable of the artist's large-scale works. Moreover, it must be noted that Miró often combines amiable with malignant forms, and in this connection Clement Greenberg's words are pertinent: "Miró's art belongs, one can say, to the Grotesque, which Ruskin defined as 'composed of two elements, one ludicrous, the other fearful.' Miró extracts amusement from the fearful, provides amusement through the fearful. As it contains a larger proportion of humor than of terror... it can be called, to quote Ruskin again, 'jesting' Grotesque. Miró sports with his fears, and the very element of sportiveness implies the decorative, ornamental, elaborate..."[37]

In 1939 Miró left Paris to take refuge from the war at Varengeville-sur-Mer, where he painted a number of small and astonishingly playful pictures on canvas and burlap (pages 102 and 103). On the fall of France, he went to Barcelona and thence to Palma, Mallorca, his wife's native town and now his permanent home. During the war only an occasional word from him arrived in this country, but none of his friends doubted that he was working incessantly, as he has worked since the beginning of his career, in war and peace, in poverty and now at last in affluence.

At this point in his career, Miró was much preoccupied with music, nature, and the texture of the surfaces on which he worked. He himself has put the matter clearly in his interview with James Sweeney: "At Varengeville-sur-Mer, in 1939, began a new stage in my work... It was about the time when the war broke out. I felt a deep desire to escape. I closed myself within myself purposely. The night, music, and the stars began to play a major role in suggesting my paintings. Music had always appealed to me, and now music in this period began to take the role poetry had played in the early twenties, especially Bach and Mozart, when I went back to Majorca upon the fall of France. Also the material of my painting began to take a new importance..."[38] At this time, too, he read enormously and was particularly fond of the Spanish mystics, St. John of the Cross and St. Theresa. And he grew fascinated by the light coming in the windows of the Gothic cathedral at Palma. He would sit there for a long time after lunch, when the cathedral was usually empty, watching the light and listening to the rolling strains of the organ. In brief, he was immersed in meditation and in absorbing such sensory impressions as those provided by music, poetry, and the more tangible stimuli of light's reflections on water and on the cathedral walls.

The result of this intense withdrawal into himself was a breathtaking series of twenty-three small gouaches, begun at Varangeville and completed at Palma, where he remained until 1942.[39]

Of these gouaches one was given by the artist to his wife; the remaining twenty-two were shown after the war at the Pierre Matisse Gallery, New York, where they had an immense and well-deserved success. The pictures in the series seem so spontaneous that it comes as a surprise to learn from Miró himself that they were "exacting both technically and physically," and that each took at least a month to produce.[40] The artist adds that he was most of all intent on compositional balance. "I would set out with no preconceived idea. A few forms suggested here would call for other forms elsewhere to balance them. These in turn demanded others... I would take it [each

Head of a Woman. August 5, 1938. Oil on canvas, $18 \times 21^5/_8''$. Collection Mr. and Mrs. Donald Winston, Los Angeles

A Drop of Dew Falling from the Wing of a Bird Awakening Rosalie Asleep in the Shadow of a Cobweb ("Goute de rosée tombant de l'aile d'un oiseau réveillant Rosalie endormie à l'ombre d'une toile d'araignée"). (1939). Oil on burlap, $25^1/_2 \times 36^1/_2$". University of Iowa, Iowa City

Woman and Kite among the Constellations. December 1939. Oil on burlap, 31⁷/₈ × 23⁵/₈″. Collection Mrs. Hildegard Ault Tjeder, New York

Left: *Awakening at Dawn*. January 27, 1941. Gouache on paper, 18 × 15″. Collection Mr. and Mrs. Ralph F. Colin, New York

Below: *Wounded Personage*. March 27, 1940. Gouache on paper, 15 × 18″. Collection Dr. and Mrs. Ernest Zeisler, Chicago

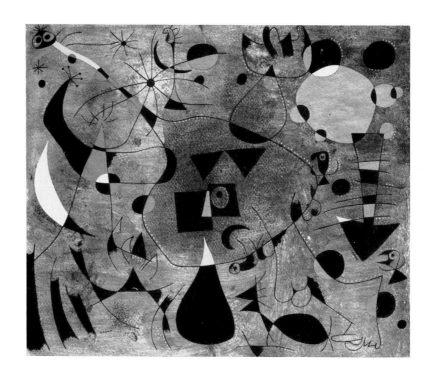

Left: *Women by the Lake with an Iridescent Surface, after the Passage of a Swan. ("Femmes au bord du lac à la surface irisée par le passage d'un cygne . . .")* May 5, 1941. Gouache on paper, 18 × 15". Mrs. James Laughlin, Norfolk, Connecticut

Right: *The Beautiful Bird Revealing the Unknown to a Pair of Lovers (Le bel oiseau déchiffrant l'inconnu au couple d'amoureaux).* July 23, 1941. Gouache on paper, 18 × 15". The Museum of Modern Art, New York, acquired through the Lillie P. Bliss Bequest

gouache] up day after day to paint in other tiny spots, stars, washes, infinitesimal dots of color in order to achieve a full and complex equilibrium."[41]

It must be admitted that seldom in his career has Miró achieved a more intricate compositional balance than in the "constellations," of which three of the finest are *The Poetess*, *Awakening at Dawn*, and *Beautiful Bird Revealing the Unknown to a Pair of Lovers* (pages 104, 105, 107). The series as a whole is extraordinary in quality, and nearly all its pictures have the signature of total conviction. These paintings also have impressive carrying power for works executed on so small a scale; the tiny forms interlock and unravel with a delicious inevitability. The most eloquent and poetic description of the "constellations" series has been given by André Breton:

"The path described from Varengeville to Palma de Mallorca between May and September 1940 only spans the two shores with a barely perceptible bridge, though one supported by unshakable conviction. One recalls without dwelling on it, appropriately, the migrations of these birds which Miró so loved to depict that one imagines they lived in him as in a tree, and that when they must depart, this tree uproots itself to move also to meet them. A statement of Prof. A. Portmann on September 12, 1958, in *Die Weltwoche* of Zurich discloses—he says one has only known about it for two years—that for example the warbler possesses an innate sense which relates it in such a way with the firmament that it is capable of directing itself without previous experience following the constellations. A large part of the winged tribe appears in command of this same gift at least, since a new generation of butterflies is considered to take the place of the old on the long journey, though their time of hatching is after the latter's decease. The word constellations which Miró employed is thus by far the most charged both with the idea of passage and of transmission in their most complete sense, both in Nature and in Myth."[42]

When the "constellations" were finished at last in Palma, Miró moved to Barcelona, where as respite from his precise concentration on the gouaches he worked very quickly and on a larger scale, as in the sumptuous *Woman and Birds in front of the Sun* (page 109). In 1944, with the war slowly and painfully reaching a breaking point, the artist completed a number of small and bold little pictures on burlap, among them the *Woman and Bird under the Moon* (page 108). And this same year he painted an abstraction over an existing realistic portrait which he had probably found in a junk shop (page 108). Some time later he was to repeat this hauntingly successful experiment on a much larger scale, as though he found satisfaction in giving vitality to an academic image in the photographic tradition.

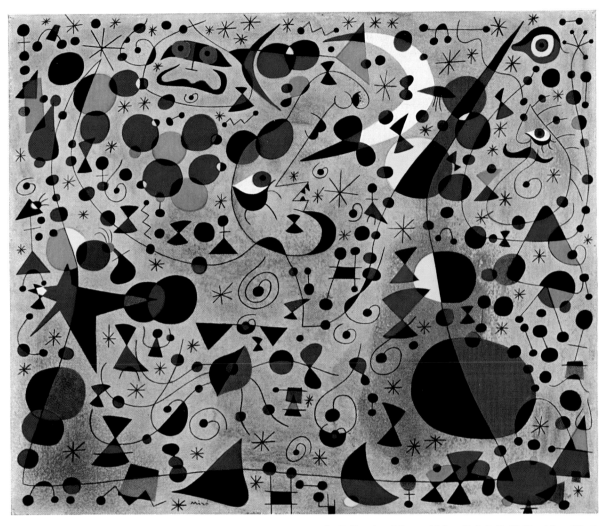

The Poetess. December 31, 1940. Gouache on paper, 15 × 18″. Collection Mr. and Mrs. Ralph F. Colin, New York

Left: *Woman and Bird under the Moon*. 1944. Oil on burlap, $8^5/_8 \times 6^1/_2''$. The Baltimore Museum of Art, Saidie A. May Collection

Below: *Personage in the Night*. 1944. Oil on canvas, $6^1/_2 \times 9^1/_8''$. Pierre Matisse Gallery, New York

Woman and Birds in front of the Sun. (1942). Gouache and pastel, $42^3/_4 \times 30^3/_4$". The Art Institute of Chicago, Wirt D. Walker Fund

Bird. (1945). Bronze, 7^1/$_2$" high. Collection Mr. and Mrs. Eliot Noyes, New Canaan, Conn.

THE MID-FORTIES: CERAMICS WITH ARTIGAS; PAINTINGS

In 1938 Miró had declared: "I would like to try sculpture, pottery, engraving, and to have a printing press. To try to go further than easel painting which in my opinion sets itself a narrow aim–to try to go as far as possible..."[43] Six years later he began to make ceramics in collaboration with José Lloréns Artigas, the celebrated potter whom he had met in 1915 in the drawing classes of Saint Luke Academy in Barcelona and whose work for Raoul Dufy and other painters he probably knew. According to Miró himself, he had tried his hand alone at ceramics much earlier: "As long ago as 1922, on my farm at Montroig near Tarragona, I made sculpture based on natural shapes–stones, plants... Later these were cast in plaster, [and] served as models for my first ceramics."[44]

The writer has never seen any of Miró's ceramics of the 1920s, but there can be little doubt that he now benefitted greatly from Artigas' expert assistance. Nevertheless, it must be said that the ceramics the two men created in the mid-1940s (below), though infinitely superior to the usual run of pottery, are less exciting than the ceramics Miró did in 1953–56, again with Artigas (pages 135–137). The difference, one assumes, is that in his earliest collaborative ceramics, Miró merely decorated the surfaces of various receptacles whose forms were invented by Artigas. (Picasso, too, had at first used established pottery shapes.) But gradually and with rising fantasy of mind, the artist began himself to create his own pottery in unconventional and non-utilitarian shapes, beginning in the 1940s with a few heads and plaques and proceeding in the next decade to what are really sculptures rather than traditional containers. As Pierre Gassier has put the matter, "Meanwhile there remained one more step to take, an audacity which Miró relishes and which is not yet known: there remained leaving to Chance the task of creating forms and to entrust them to the ceramist with all the fantasy of cracks, flaws, protuberances, and gashes. Just as Miró loves to pick up from the path a stone, a root, or a twisted piece of scrap-iron whose unexpected forms seem to have cried out to him in the name of some strange beauty, so he selects

 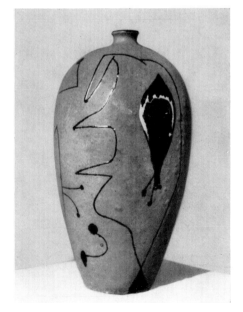

Miró and Artigas: Left: *Ceramic*. (1945). 7^1/$_8$ × 4". Right: *Vase*. (1945). Ceramic, 15^5/$_8$" high. Both: Pierre Matisse Gallery, New York

Women Listening to Music. (1945). Oil on canvas, 51 × 64″. Collection Mrs. Evelyn Sharp, New York

A Ballet Dancer Listening to Organ Music in a Gothic Cathedral. May 5, 1945. Oil on canvas, 77 × 51 1/2″. Collection Mr. and Mrs. Keith Warner, Norwich, Vermont

Woman and Bird in the Night. March 8, 1945. Oil on canvas, 51 × 64″. Albright Art Gallery, Buffalo, gift of Seymour H. Knox

he Harbor. July 2, 1945. Oil on canvas, $51^{1}/_{8} \times 63^{3}/_{4}''$. Collection Mr. and Mrs. Armand P. Bartos, New York

Spanish Dancer. July 7, 1945. Oil on canvas, $57^1/_2 \times 44^7/_8''$. Collection Mr. and Mrs. Daniel Saidenberg, New York

Women in the Night. June 11, 1946. Oil on canvas, 13 × 25¹/₄″. Collection Mr. and Mrs. Niels Onstad, New York

from a heap of debris, fragments of pottery or glass, the piece worthy in its turn to become a 'support.' The game of Chance thus preceded that of Fire and between the two, in the heart of the most elementary hidden forces that exist, is Miró's intervention, reduced to a minimum, a simple flash of creative conscience."[45]

The superiority of the 1953–56 series of ceramics has been acknowledged by Artigas: "Miró had been seeking to express his imagination and invention through new techniques. It was my job, as a technician, to provide him with the broadest scope of possibilities in my field. We made a start when we first worked together, but this last group carried us much further."[46] And Miró himself has testified to his interest in transcending the utilitarian or purely decorative basis of the usual ceramic forms: "Some of them [the ceramics of 1953–56] are very big – 12 feet high, 9 feet, or 4. The large pieces are meant for out-of-doors. I worked in a monumental spirit, thinking of a possible association with architecture – not to treat men who must live in modern buildings like unfeeling robots."[47] Moreover, it is more than clear from what Miró and others have said that he and Artigas exploited those very accidents of procedure which it is the business of conventional potters to avoid: "It's impossible to repeat the same thing twice: exactly the same degree of heat and length of time in the oven will produce different results. Nothing is foreseeable – the smoke, the quality of the fire, can change a nuance. Sometimes 'accidents' in baking would suggest a new idea to me. What had started out to be a vegetable form would be distorted in a way that made me think of a face: I would add a nose and a bit here and there, and it would turn into a human figure. There was a constant metamorphosis – a thing that started out with one identity grew into another."[48] This metamorphosis is apparent in many of the roughly two hundred pieces Miró executed between 1953 and 1956. The best of them have made him a not unworthy rival to his great countryman, Picasso, at the art of ceramics.

During much of 1945 Miró lived in Artigas' house at Gallifa, and a great part of his time was naturally spent on ceramics rather than paintings. Nevertheless, a number of important pictures date from this year. They fall into two rough categories: those in which linear forms are predominant, as in *The Harbor*, *Spanish Dancer*, and *Woman and Bird in the Night* (pages 114–116); and those in which the color is quite densely organized, as in *Women Listening to Music* and *Ballet Dancer Listening to Organ Music in a Gothic Cathedral* (pages 112 and 113). In the first-named series Miró seems to have been primarily concerned with creating ideograms, as the Chinese had been long before him. Indeed, the relationship of Miró's later art to Oriental traditions has been commented on by several critics. Yet this art's character remains essentially Spanish or, more specifically, Catalan, and its purposeful naivete and childlike humor are far removed from the elegant sophistication of the Chinese masters.

The *Women Listening to Music* now hangs in the bar of the Stanhope Hotel in New York, and has had the curious if harmlessly gratifying distinction of having had some of its forms transferred to such appurtenances of the barroom as ashtrays, match covers, and paper coasters. Its composition, like that of its companion piece, the *Ballet Dancer Listening to Organ Music in a Gothic Cathedral*, is masterfully planned in large dark areas, relieved by aggressive accents of white, red, yellow, and green. Both works are decoration of a very high order, and are therefore remembered as much larger than they actually are. It is interesting to speculate on how much both pictures

Opposite: *Woman and Little Girl in front of the Sun*. Nov. 30 – Dec. 19, 1946. Oil on canvas, $57^3/_8 \times 44^7/_8''$. Private collection, New York

Women at Sunrise. June 17, 1946. Oil on canvas, 15 × 24″. Nelson Gallery – Atkins Museum, Kansas City (Friends of Art Collection)

were affected by the colors and forms of the stained-glass windows in the cathedral where Miró had sat so often.

In 1946 Miró painted the *Women at Sunrise* (above) and *The Night* (opposite), the latter exploiting at its center those wavery, unpremeditated smears of which the artist is fond, the former uniformly precise in texture and line. At this time he also completed the beguiling little *Women in the Night* (page 117) which suggests a preparatory plan for a mural such as Miró was to create for Cincinnati's Terrace Hilton Hotel the following year. And at the very end of 1946 Miró finished the *Woman and Little Girl in front of the Sun* (page 119), a picture in which we are made fully aware of that strange interplay between careful definition and casual effects which occurs in so many of the painter's works of recent years. The two central figures are concisely outlined against a pearly ground. Then at the right there is a dark form, suggesting a man with sombrero, which in its uncalculated spontaneity puts one in mind of finger painting. At the bottom left a white splotch of heavy pigment adds an impulsive liveliness to the

The Night. February 22, 1946. Oil on canvas, 23³/₄ × 28³/₄″. Collection Mr. and Mrs. LeRoy Make-peace, Waterbury, Connecticut

image as a whole. The workings of Miró's imaginative process are mysterious and unpredictable. We know, for example, that in one instance he centered an otherwise painstaking composition around an accidental splash of blackberry jam.[49] As he himself has said, "Even a few casual wipes of my brush in cleaning it may suggest the beginning of a picture. The second stage, however, is carefully calculated. The first stage is free, unconscious; but after that the picture is controlled throughout, in keeping with that desire for disciplined work I have felt from the beginning."[50]

1947–51: THE CINCINNATI AND HARVARD MURALS; PAINTINGS

In 1947 Miró was commissioned to paint for the Gourmet Restaurant of the new Terrace Hilton Hotel in Cincinnati, Ohio, a mural (above) measuring roughly seven by thirty-two feet.[51] He came to America expressly for the purpose, and in the studio of the American painter, Carl Holty, on East 119th Street, New York City, worked on the mural for a period of months. Painted on a soft blue ground, the mural was to become a virtual anthology of the forms, mostly in red, yellow, green, and black, by which Miró had been engrossed for some time. The mural's gaiety and sweep are most impressive, though the melancholy fact must be recorded that in its present location in the restaurant, its headlong arabesques are arrested at impertinent intervals by supporting columns in front of the wall. (In fairness to the hotel and its architects, it must be noted that Miró was warned beforehand that the columns were necessary, and apparently raised no objection.) The mural remains a commendable *tour de force*, the more so in that it was painted in a relatively short time, being completed and dry enough to be shipped for temporary exhibition at the Museum of Modern Art on

Mural. (1947). Oil on canvas, 6′7″×31′6″. Gourmet Restaurant, Terrace Hilton Hotel, Cincinnati. Collection Thomas Emery's Sons, Inc.

October 24, 1947. It was also painted without assistants and in a foreign city–an important factor for an artist like Miró, whose imagination feeds on the Catalan environment.

The writer, like all those who saw the artist working on the huge canvas in Holty's studio, will never forget the fervor and certainty with which Miró attacked problems of spacing and contrast, nor how easily the fantastic and personal motifs seemed to lead one to another. Here beyond question was a master decorator at work, and if the mural lacks the profundity of Miró's finest easel pictures, it nevertheless fulfills brilliantly its festive purpose.

Several years later Miró was to do still better in his mural for Harkness Commons in the Graduate Center of Harvard University, Cambridge, Mass. (pages 130–131). The mural, measuring 6 feet 2¼ inches by 19 feet 5½ inches, was approved by Harvard from a preliminary sketch (page 131) on March 14th, 1950, and was painted during the winter of 1950–51. It was shown in the Maeght Gallery, Paris, in the spring,

The Moon. 1948. Oil on canvas, 28 × 36″. Collection Mr. and Mrs. Charles Zadok, New York

and arrived at the University on June 21, 1951. Of it Miró has said that he hoped it "will enable me to establish close contact with the student, the young men of tomorrow. It is better to influence the young generation than to try to convert stubborn old men."[52]

Doubtless the fact that the mural was planned for an educational institution persuaded Miró to work with a sterner creative impetus than he had for the Cincinnati hotel's dining room wall. Another helpful factor was that this time he was able to paint in his own studio in Spain, always a consoling advantage, as noted in passing. At any rate, we can see the mural's progression toward a simplified monumentality by comparing it with its preliminary sketch. The forms in the mural are broadly organ-

Red Sun. 1948. Oil on canvas, 36×28″. The Phillips Gallery, Washington, D. C.

Personages in the Night. 1950. Oil on burlap, 35 × 45³/₄″. Collection Mr. and Mrs. Charles Zadok, New York

ized, and there is a strong plastic continuity between the various fantastic figures. The mural's effect is less playful than that of the sketch, and there is a marvelous interweaving of linear with tonal passages. And finally, whereas the protruding head at the left of the sketch tended to pull the composition to one side, now in the mural there is a deft equilibrium throughout. This assuredly is among the most impressive contemporary murals now on public display in this country.

Painting. 1949. Oil on canvas, 25³/₄×32″. Collection Mr. and Mrs. Morton G. Neumann, Chicago

Despite his absorption in two large-scale commissions, Miró also completed a number of outstanding easel paintings at this period (pages 124–127). Among them are the superbly luminous and poetic *Red Sun*, the *Painting* in the Neumann collection, whose wry protagonists stalk the evening air, and the *Personages in the Night*, with its dulcet atmospheric effects and its appealing birds with moon-like wings.

During 1950, Miró's reflections on the intricate problems of the Harvard mu-

127

Painting. 1950. Oil on canvas, 32 × 39¹/₂″. Collection Mr. and Mrs. Gordon Bunshaft, New York

Personage and Moon. 1950. Oil on canvas, 39³/₄ × 29″. Private collection, New York

Mural in Harkness Commons Dining Room, Graduate Center, Harvard University, Cambridge, Massachusetts (1950–51). Oil on canvas, 6′2¼″ × 19′5½″.

ral may have had some influence on two charming pictures of medium size, *Painting* and the *Personage and Moon* (pages 128 and 129). In the *Birds, Figures, and Blue Star* (page 132), the artist seems to have taken a backward glance at the intricate condensation and profusion of forms in the "constellation" series, and his interest in collage revived in a capital work with string and rope, the *Composition* (page 133), whose vaporous background provides a breathtakingly sensitive foil to the figures and cords painted on or affixed to the surface. In 1950, too, Miró made two sculptures in traditional materials: a large head in granite which later served as a basis for one of his most ambitious ceramics (page 135 left); and a small bronze.

Study for Harkness mural
(c. 1950). Tempera and ink,
$8\frac{1}{2} \times 24''$. Fogg Art Museum,
Cambridge, Massachusetts

Birds, Figures, and Blue Star. (1950). Oil on canvas, $51^1/_4 \times 38^1/_4''$.
Collection Mr. and Mrs. Richard Deutsch, Greenwich, Connecticut

Composition. 1950. Oil, plaster, and rope on canvas, $38 \times 29^7/_8$″. Galerie Maeght, Paris

Miró at Gallifa, 1956. Photo Sabine Weiss

THE RECENT YEARS

If during the past few years Miró has produced fewer extensive series of paintings than before, the reasons are not far to seek. To begin with, from 1953 to 1956, as already noted, he produced around two hundred ceramics with Artigas. This was a prodigious effort which may well have reached its climax of eloquence and power in the *Portico* of 1956 (page 136). In 1957 the artist had published by Louis Broder in Paris a suite of twenty-two etchings, drypoints, and aquatints entitled *La Bague d'Aurore*, many of them extremely fine. Then for a very long time he was preoccupied with making woodcuts for Paul Eluard's book of poems, *A Toute Epreuve*, originally pub-

Miró and Artigas: *Personage*. (1956). Ceramic, 39¹/₂″ high. Pierre Matisse Gallery, New York

Miró and Artigas: *Head*. 1956. Ceramic, 20¹/₂″ high. Collection Mr. and Mrs. Robert Osborn, Salisbury, Connecticut

lished without illustrations. Miró's book has now been issued and constitutes one of the most triumphant feats of book illustration in our century (page 139).

We know from Miró's correspondence with *A Toute Epreuve*'s publisher, Gérald Cramer, that the idea for the book was first broached by the latter as early as 1947. In March of that year the artist wrote Cramer as follows: "Monsieur, I have received your letter of March 8, with the brochure of Eluard, and I must tell you with what enthusiasm I am going to illustrate it."[53] He adds that it was impossible for him to begin at once, due to the pressure of working on the Cincinnati mural. On June 19, 1948, he wrote Cramer again: "New ideas for the book are always coming into my head. A few days ago at Montroig, a walk in the forest suggested the idea of using as point of departure the marvelous forms of fir roots... I have made some trials which have allowed me to see what it was to *make* a book and not merely to illustrate it. Illustration is always a secondary matter. The important thing is that a book have all the dignity of a sculpture carved in marble."[54]

Miró had already decided that his illustrations were to be woodcuts in color, a medium he felt had not been adequately explored: "As to woodcuts, of all that has been done in modern times, I can accept only Gauguin. Well, you will allow me to say that my ambition is to go still further."[55] He makes his aims more explicit in a postscript

Opposite: Miró and Artigas: *Portico.* April 1956. Nine ceramic sections, 98" high. The Solomon R. Guggenheim Museum, New York

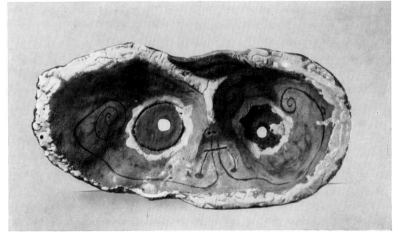

Miró and Artigas: *Head.* (1956). Ceramic, $9\frac{1}{2} \times 18$". Pierre Matisse Gallery, New York

to the same letter to Cramer: "Long conversations with a friend who stayed several years in Japan and who is himself a wood engraver, have made me see the technical riches one can obtain–preliminary preparation of the paper and pulling the proofs, apart from the style of cutting the blocks, while adding accidental engraving as an adornment."[56] It is entirely clear from other letters to Mr. and Mrs. Cramer that Miró was completely absorbed in his task, which was not finished until 1958, with exemplary help from master engravers and printers.[57] The author of the book's text, Paul Eluard, had an important part in planning the typography, though he did not, alas, live to see the work published.

Considering the quality of *A Toute Epreuve*, no one could begrudge the time Miró spent on it rather than on painting. And concurrently the artist did produce some exceptional pictures, among them *Painting* (page 142), with its brutally gouged and burnt forms, which may have been affected, however obliquely, by Miró's absorption in woodcuts at the time, the Raoul Lévy picture (page 143) and, perhaps above all, the Guggenheim Museum's *Painting* (page 140), in which Miró revived a favorite device – the encirclement of various shapes with confetti-like halos composed of small dots of color. In 1952–1953 he produced the *Red Disk in Pursuit of the Lark* (page 144) and slightly later the excellent picture (page 141), in which appears part of the jack-in-the-box that Miró delightedly plays with in a sequence from Thomas Bouchard's film on the master. The following year he painted *Hope Returns to Us through the Flight of Constellations* (page 145), with its poetic imprints of his own hands and handsome fluidity of color.

In 1955 Miró was commissioned by UNESCO's Art Committee to decorate with ceramics two walls outside its new buildings in Paris. Both walls are three meters high, the one fifteen meters long, the other seven and a half. Once more the artist chose Artigas as his collaborator. The murals took more than three years to complete, and Miró has written a detailed account of his and Artigas' labors. The larger wall is entitled *Day*, the smaller one *Night* (page 146).

Miró makes clear that he first of all took into consideration the surrounding architecture: "The very forms of the buildings, their spatial organization, the conditions of light, have suggested the forms and colors of my walls. I wished to incorporate my work with the ensemble, while seeking a contrast with the architecture. Thus in reaction against the concrete slabs which surround it, the idea of a huge disk in powerful red occurred to me for the large wall. Its rejoinder on the small wall would be a blue crescent, dictated by the more restrained and intimate space for which

Illustrations for *A Toute Epreuve*, a book by Paul Eluard (bibl. 29). Page size $12^5/_8 \times 9^7/_8{}''$.
The Museum of Modern Art, New York, gift of Mr. and Mrs. Walter Bareiss

Painting. (1953). Oil on canvas, 6'4³/₄" × 12'4³/₄". The Solomon R. Guggenheim Museum, New York

it was intended. These two forms, which I wanted to be intense in color, had to be still further reinforced by hollowed-out passages. Detailed elements of the construction, such as the placing of the windows, have inspired me to create checkered compositions and figures. I sought a brutal expression in the large wall, a more poetic one in the smaller. Within each composition I sought at the same time a contrast by opposing to the black, ferocious and dynamic drawing, calm colored forms, flat or in squares."[58]

Miró adds that in creating the ceramic walls he and Artigas had four main sources of inspiration: an old corroded wall in the Romanesque church, the "Collegiata," at Santillana in Spain; the paleolithic wall paintings at Altamira; the Romanesque frescoes in the Barcelona museum; and, in Gaudí's Park Güell, "an immense disk prepared

Painting. (1953). Oil on canvas,
75 7/8 × 51″. Collection Mr. and Mrs.
Richard K. Weil, St. Louis

Painting. (1953). Oil on masonite, $42^1/_2 \times 21^1/_4''$.
Collection Mr. and Mrs. G. David Thompson,
Pittsburgh

Coiffeur Disheveled by the Flight of Constellations ("La Chevelure défaite à la fuite des constellations . . .") 1954. Oil on tapestry, $51 \times 70\frac{1}{4}''$.
Collection M. and Mme Raoul Lévy, Paris

The Red Disk in Pursuit of the Lark (*"Le disque rouge à la poursuite de l'alouette . . ."*) (1952–53). Oil on canvas, 51 × 37³/₄". Galerie Maeght, Paris

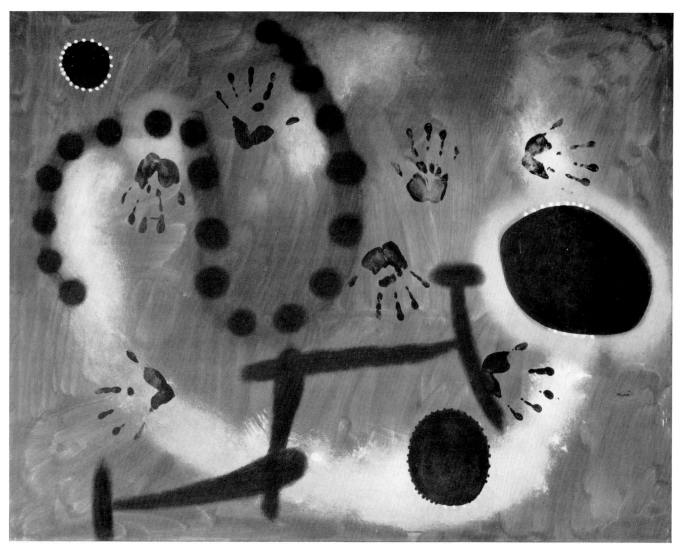

Hope Returns to Us through the Flight of Constellations ("L'Espoir nous revient par la fuite des constellations . . ."). 1954. Oil on canvas, 44⁷/₈ × 57¹/₂". Galerie Maeght, Paris

Miró and Artigas: *Night*. (1955–58). Ceramic, 9′10″ × 24′6″. Wall commissioned for UNESCO headquarters, Place de Fontenoy, Paris

in the wall itself and revealing the bare rock, entirely like that which I proposed to engrave and paint on [my] large wall."[59] The trip which Miró and Artigas made to visit these monuments of native art of the past gave them the necessary vision to begin the two walls for UNESCO. But their progress was by no means straightforward and certain, and at one point they began one wall all over again since Artigas, and presumably Miró as well, was dissatisfied with the surfaces they had obtained by comparison with those they kept seeing on the walls of the old church at Gallifa, where they were working in Artigas' studio.

The last ceramics for UNESCO were placed in the kilns on May 29, 1958. Previously no less than thirty-four bakings had been required, all of them over wood fires since, as Miró declares, "cooking with wood permits effects which one can not obtain with gas, charcoal, or electricity."[60] The ceramic walls have since been installed at their intended site on the Place de Fontenoy in Paris, where they have provoked a mixed but on the whole enthusiastic reaction among art critics and architects, with the latter more reticent in their praise than the former. Since the writer has never seen the murals themselves, no comment will be made here except to note that this was a stupendous undertaking, requiring boundless energy and patience.

Energy and patience! To Miró, now in his sixty-seventh year, many comparable words could be applied without strain, even the most flattering and extravagant. Whether in paintings, ceramics, or prints, he works still with the abandon of youth and with youth's defiant assurance. Today he is as free in invention as at any time in his long career. His international fame and the adulation of many have done nothing to spoil his simplicity as a man nor to dull his exalted aims, both cautious and wild, as an artist. He now writes and speaks of himself with quiet dignity. But also with wonder, as though his gifts awed him more than a little. His creative volition drives him on ceaselessly. No doubt we shall see many more inimitable works of art from his star-struck hand.

NOTES TO THE TEXT

1 *Minotaure*, No. 3, 1933, p. 18.

2 James Johnson Sweeney, "Joan Miró: Comment and Interview," *Partisan Review*, No. 2, February 1948, p. 210 [hereinafter referred to as Sweeney interview].

3 Joan Miró, "Je rêve d'un grand atelier," *XX Siècle*, No. 2, May 1938, p. 28.

4 Rosamond Bernier, "Miró the Ceramist," *The Selective Eye*, 1956–57, p. 9.

5 *Ibid.*, p. 12.

6 Sweeney interview, p. 209.

7 *Ibid.*, p. 209.

8 *Ibid.*, p. 208.

9 Jacques Viot, "Un Ami: Joan Miró," *Cahiers d'Art*, No. 8–10, 1936, p. 257.

10 Edouard Roditi, "Interview with Joan Miró," *Arts*, Vol. 33, No. I, October 1958, p. 43.

11 Clement Greenberg, *Joan Miró*, The Quadrangle Press, New York, 1948, p. 13.

12 Georges Duthuit, "Où allez-vous Miró," *Cahiers d'Art*, No. 8–10, 1936, p. 262.

13 Georges Hugnet, "Joan Miró ou l'enfance de l'art," *Cahiers d'Art*, No. 7–8, 1931, p. 336.

14 Ernest Hemingway, "The Farm," *Cahiers d'Art*, Nos. 1–4, 1934, p. 28.

15 Hugnet, *op. cit.*, p. 338.

16 Alfred H. Barr, Jr., ed., *Masters of Modern Art*, The Museum of Modern Art, New York, 1954, p. 142.

17 André Breton, *Le surréalisme et la peinture*, Brentano's, New York, 1945, p. 68.

18 *Ibid.*, p. 94.

19 Reproduced in *Collection of the Société Anonyme: Museum of Modern Art 1920*, Yale University Art Gallery, New Haven, Conn., 1950, p. 109.

20 Sweeney interview, p. 209.

21 André Breton, "Surrealism," *This Quarter*, Vol. 5, No. 1, Sept. 1932, p. 16.

22 *Ibid.*, p. 16.

23 René Gaffé, "Joan Miró," *Cahiers d'Art*, Nos. 1–4, 1930, p. 30.

24 James Johnson Sweeney, "Miro," *Art News Annual*, Vol. XXIII, 1954, p. 71.

25 Roditi, *op. cit.*, p. 41.

26 Greenberg, *op. cit.*, p. 31.

27 Christian Zervos, "Joan Miró," *Cahiers d'Art*, Nos. 1–4, 1934, p. 14.

28 Miró's unease in working for the theatre may well have been heightened by the fact that Surrealism's leaders, Breton and Louis Aragon, had tried bitterly to dissuade Ernst and himself from accepting the commission to do the decor for *Roméo et Juliette*. For these leaders, the ballet was the decadent concern of "the international aristocracy."

29 Sweeney interview, p. 210.

30 Barr, *op. cit.*, p. 142.

31 This object has been identified by Miró himself as an apple, not a potato or squash.

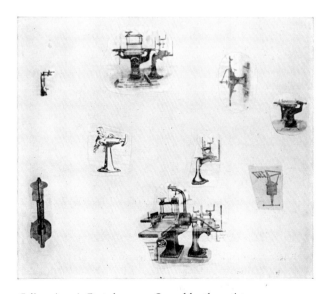

Collage. (1933). Pasted papers. Owned by the artist

Left: Raphael (1483–1520):
La Fornarina. Barbarini Palace, Rome.
(Gab. Fot. Naz. – Roma)

Right: Jean Arp (born 1887):
Madame Torso with Wavy Hat. 1916.
Wood, 15⁷/₈ × 10³/₈″. Collection
Hermann Rupf, Bern

32 James Johnson Sweeney, *Joan Miro*, The Museum of Modern Art, New York, 1941, p. 68.

33 Juan Larrea, ″Miroir d'Espagne,″ *Cahiers d'Art*, Nos. 4–5, 1937, p. 158.

34 Peter Watson, ″Joan Miró,″ *Horizon*, London, Vol. IV, No. 20, August 1941, pp. 132–133.

35 Roger Hauert and André Verdet, *Joan Miró*, Kister, Geneva, 1956, p. 20.

36 *Ibid.*, p. 19.

37 Greenberg, *op. cit.*, p. 42.

38 Sweeney interview, p. 210.

39 The first picture in the series was completed on January 21, 1940, the last on September 12, 1941.

40 Sweeney interview, p. 211.

41 *Ibid.*, p. 211.

42 André Breton, ″Constellations de Joan Miró,″ *L'Oeil*, No. 48, December 1958, pp. 52, 55.

43 Miró, ″Je rêve d'un grand atelier,″ *op. cit.*, p. 28.

44 Rosamond Bernier, ″Miró céramiste,″ *L'Oeil*, No. 17, May 1956, p. 46. (In this article both Miró and Artigas have said that they began their ceramics in 1945, but the former has since corrected this date to 1944.)

45 Pierre Gassier, ″Miró et Artigas,″ *Labyrinthe*, Vol. II, Nos. 22–23, December 1946, p. 11.

46 Rosamond Bernier, ″Miró the Ceramist,″ *The Selective Eye*, 1956–57, p. 6.

47 *Ibid.*, p. 6.

48 *Ibid.*, pp. 11, 12.

49 Sweeney interview, p. 212.

50 *Ibid.*, p. 212.

51 The mural is destined for the Cincinnati Art Museum.

52 *Time*, July 10, 1950, p. 45.

53 Joan Miró, letters to Mr. and Mrs. Cramer. Photostats of the correspondence are on file in the Museum's Library.

54 *Ibid.*

55 *Ibid.*

56 *Ibid.*

57 Jacques Frélaut and Jaime Herrera.

58 Joan Miró, ″Ma dernière œuvre est un mur,″ *Derrière le Miroir*, Paris, p. 24.

59 *Ibid.*, p. 25.

60 *Ibid.*, p. 25.

LIST OF EXHIBITIONS

The following modifies the list reported in the Museum's monograph (bibl. 44) and in the documentation prepared by Hannah Muller, formerly on the Library staff (bibl. 35), with subsequent selective additions. *Sylvia Hill*

1918 BARCELONA. Galerie Dalmau. Feb. 16 to Mar. 3.

1921 PARIS. Galerie La Licorne. Apr. 29 to May 14. See bibl. 175.

1923 PARIS. Caméléon Club. September. Cited Cirlot bibl. 33.

1925 PARIS. Galerie Pierre. June 12 to 27. Organized by Jacques Viot.

1925 PARIS. Galerie Pierre. Nov. 14 to 25.

1928 PARIS. Galerie Georges Bernheim et Cie. May 1 to 15. Organized by the Galerie Pierre.

1929 BRUSSELS. Galerie Le Centaure. May 11 to 23.

1930 PARIS. Galerie Goemans. March. See bibl. 176.

1930 PARIS. Galerie Pierre. May 7 to 22.

1930 NEW YORK. The Valentine Gallery. Oct. 20 to Nov. 8.

1931 CHICAGO. The Arts Club of Chicago. Jan. 27 to Feb. 17.

1931 PARIS. Galerie Pierre. Dec. 18, 1931 to Jan. 8, 1932.

1931 NEW YORK. The Valentine Gallery. Dec. 28, 1931 to Jan. 16, 1932.

1932 NEW YORK. Pierre Matisse Gallery. Nov. 1 to 25.

1932 PARIS. Galerie Pierre Colle. Dec. 13 to 16.

1933 LONDON. The Mayor Gallery. July.

1933 PARIS. Galerie Georges Bernheim et Cie. Oct. 30 to Nov. 13. Organized by the Galerie Pierre.

1933 NEW YORK. Pierre Matisse Gallery. Dec. 29, 1933 to Jan. 18, 1934.

1934 CHICAGO. The Arts Club of Chicago. Mar. 16 to 30. Cited Cirlot bibl. 33.

1934 PARIS. Galerie des Cahiers d'Art. May 3 to 19. Organized by Yvonne Zervos.

1934 SAN FRANCISCO. East-West Gallery. June. Organized by Howard Putzel. Cited Cirlot bibl. 33.

1935 NEW YORK. Pierre Matisse Gallery. Jan. 10 to Feb. 9.

1935 SAN FRANCISCO. San Francisco Museum of Art. June 30 to Aug. 12, and Dec. 1 to 15. Cited Cirlot bibl. 33.

1935 LOS ANGELES. Stendahl Gallery. September.

1935 HOLLYWOOD. Stanley Rose Gallery. Oct. 14 to Nov. 2. Organized by Howard Putzel.

1936 LONDON. New Burlington Galleries. June 11–July 4. See bibl. 177.

1936 NEW YORK. Pierre Matisse Gallery. Nov. 30 to Dec. 26.

1937 HOLLYWOOD. Stegel Antheil Gallery. March. Cited Cirlot bibl. 33.

1937 HOLLYWOOD. Putzel Gallery. March. Cited Cirlot bibl. 33.

1937 LONDON. The Zwemmer Gallery. May 6 to June 2.

1937 TOKYO. Nippon Salon. June. See bibl. 178.

1937 HONOLULU. Honolulu Academy of Arts. Summer. Cited Cirlot bibl. 33.

1938 NEW YORK. Pierre Matisse Gallery. Apr. 18 to May 7.

1938 LONDON. Mayor Gallery. May 4 to 28. See bibl. 179.

1938 CHICAGO. Katherine Kuh Galleries. Nov. 1 to 30.

1939 LONDON. London Gallery (with Louis Marcoussis). Apr. 14 to 27. Organized by E. L. T. Mesens. Cited Cirlot bibl. 33.

1939 NEW YORK. Pierre Matisse Gallery. Apr. 10 to May 6.

1940 NEW YORK. Pierre Matisse Gallery. Mar. 12 to 31. See bibl. 180.

1940 NEW YORK. Gallery of Living Art. (N.Y.U.) See bibl. 181, 193.

1941 RICHMOND. Virginia Museum of Fine Arts. Jan. 16 to Mar. 4. See bibl. 183.

1941 NEW YORK. Pierre Matisse Gallery. Mar. 4 to 29.

1941 NEW YORK. The Museum of Modern Art. Nov. 18, 1941 to Jan. 11, 1942. See bibl. 182. Later circulated to Smith College, Vassar College, Portland Art Museum, San Francisco Museum of Art.

1942 NEW YORK. Art of This Century. Nov. See bibl. 184.

1942 NEW YORK. Pierre Matisse Gallery. Dec. 8 to 31.

1943 CHICAGO. Arts Club of Chicago. Mar. 24 to Apr. 7.

1944 NEW YORK. Pierre Matisse Gallery. May 3 to June 3.

1945 NEW YORK. Pierre Matisse Gallery. Jan. 9 to Feb. 3.

1945 NEW YORK. Pierre Matisse Gallery. Feb. 5 to 25.

1945 PARIS. Galerie Vendôme. Mar. 27 to Apr. 28.

1946 BOSTON. Institute of Contemporary Art. Jan. 24 to Mar. 3. (With Dali, Gris, Picasso.)

1947 NEW YORK. Pierre Matisse Gallery. May 13 to June 7.

1947 PARIS. Galerie Maeght. July. See bibl. 185.

1948 NEW YORK. Museum of Modern Art. Mar. 3 to Apr. 4. (Mural for Terrace Plaza Hotel, Cincinnati.)

1948 NEW YORK. Pierre Matisse Gallery. Mar. 16 to Apr. 10.

1948 LONDON. Zwemmer Gallery. Beginning May 25. (With Borès and Picasso.)

1948 SAN FRANCISCO. San Francisco Museum of Art. Sept. 14 to Oct. 17. See bibl. 186.

1948 PORTLAND, ORE. Portland Art Museum. Oct. 26 to Nov. 28. See bibl. 186.

1948 PARIS. Galerie Maeght. Nov. 19 to Dec. 18. See bibl. 118.

1949 LONDON. Institute of Contemporary Art. Dec. 20, 1948 to Jan. 29, 1949. See bibl. 190.

1949 STOCKHOLM. Galerie Blanche. Apr. 9 to May 3.

1949 NEW YORK. Pierre Matisse Gallery. Apr. 19 to May 14.

1949 BERN. Kunsthalle. Apr. 21 to May 29. See bibl. 188.

1949 BARCELONA. Galerias Layetans. Apr. 23 to May 6. See bibl. 117.

1949 BASEL. Kunsthalle. June 14 to July 17.

1949 NEW YORK. Perspectives Gallery. October.

1949 CHICAGO. Art Institute. Oct. 20 to Dec. 18. See bibl. 189.

1949 NEW YORK. Pierre Matisse Gallery. Dec. 6 to 31.

1950 LONDON. London Gallery. Feb. 2 to 28.

1950 PARIS. Galerie Maeght. May and June. See bibl. 118.

1950 STOCKHOLM. Galerie Blanche. [November.]

1951 NEW YORK. Pierre Matisse Gallery. Mar. 6 to 31.

1951 NEW YORK. Pierre Matisse Gallery. Nov. 20 to Dec. 15.

1952 NEW YORK. Kootz Gallery. Jan. 28 to Feb. 16. (With Vlaminck and Léger.)

1952 NEW YORK. Pierre Matisse Gallery. Apr. 15 to May 17.

1952 SAARBRUCK. La Mission Diplomatique Française en Sarre. Summer. (La peinture surréaliste en Europe.)

1952 BASEL. Kunsthalle. Aug. 30 to Oct. 12.

1953 PARIS. Galerie Maeght. June to Aug. See bibl. 118.

1953 BERN. Kunsthalle. July 31 to Sept. 20.

1953 NEW YORK. Pierre Matisse Gallery. Nov. 17 to Dec. 12. See bibl. 192.

1954 KREFELD. Kaiser Wilhelm Museum. January. See bibl. 194.

1954 NEW YORK. Galerie Chalette. Feb. 16 to Mar. 13.

1954 STUTTGART. Staatsgalerie. Feb. 21 to Mar. 28.

1954 MINNEAPOLIS. Walker Art Center. May 23 to July 2.

1954 VENICE. XXVII Biennale. June 19 to Oct. 17.

1955 KASSEL. Museum Fridericianum. July 15 to Sept. 18.

1955 LAUSANNE. Musée Cantonal des Beaux-Arts. June 24 to Sept. 26.

1955 NEW YORK. Brooklyn Museum. Oct. 31 to Nov. 14. (Prints-Fabrics by Picasso, Miró, Chagall, Léger, Dufy.)

1955 NEW YORK. Pierre Matisse Gallery. December.

1956 BRUSSELS. Palais des Beaux-Arts. Jan. 6 to Feb. 7. See bibl. 195, 197.

1956 ANTWERP. Zaal C.A.W. Apr. 15 to 26. (With Magritte, Tanguy, Ernst.)

1956 PARIS. Galerie Maeght. June to August. See bibl. 197.

1956 NEW YORK. Pierre Matisse Gallery. Dec. 4 to 30. See bibl. 198.

1957 KREFELD. Kaiser Wilhelm Museum. April. See bibl. 199.

1957 NEW YORK. Knoedler & Company. Apr. 2 to 20. See bibl. 201.

1957 SAINT GALLEN. Kunstverein. Aug. 3 to Oct. 20.

1957 HANOVER. Kestner-Gesellschaft. Dec. 11 to Jan. 19, 1958. See bibl. 200.

1958 HOUSTON. Contemporary Arts Museum. Jan. 9 to Feb. 16.

1958 NEW YORK. Museum of Modern Art. Jan. 29 to Mar. 2. (Prints, with Braque and Morandi.)

1958 PARIS. Galerie Berggruen. Apr. 25 to June 5.

1958 BRUSSELS. Palais des Beaux-Arts. Apr. 17 to July 21.

1958 PARIS. Galerie Maeght. June to July. See bibl. 118.

1958 AIX-EN-PROVENCE. Pavillon de Vendôme. July 15 to Sept. 28.

1958 LIÈGE. Musée de L'Art Walloon. July to Sept. See bibl. 202.

1958 CLEVELAND. Howard Wise Gallery. Sept. 7–30.

1958 NEW YORK. Pierre Matisse Gallery. Nov. 4 to 29. See bibl. 203.

1959 NEW YORK. F.A.R. Gallery. Jan. 5 to 24. (Lithographs and etchings.)

1959 PARIS. Galerie Berggruen. Jan. 16–Mar. (Constellations.)

BIBLIOGRAPHY

A considerable amount of documentation already exists on this Spanish artist, which makes it advisable, in the present instance, to organize an evaluated and classified body of references. In addition to the more comprehensive listing in the Bern catalogue (bibl. 188) and the studies by Greenberg (bibl. 35) and Prévert (bibl. 40), the serious reader will find additional specialized data in bibls. 42, 44, 71, 87, 99, 112, 119, 191. The "select bibliography" in Hunter (bibl. 36) is actually an extensive but incomplete list of Miró's graphics which intermingles print editions and illustrated items. Other inventories exist (bibl. 48, 96) and supply supplementary data. The graphic selections (bibl. 21–30) represent characteristic works in different fields, illustrating the artist's technical range and invention, as well as a cherished affinity for his literary colleagues: the poets. Adequate references to the surrealist literature itself will be found in Barr (bibl. 52) and Nadeau (bibl. 101).

Bernard Karpel
Librarian of the Museum

TEXTS BY MIRO

1 [Declaraciones]. *Cobalto 49 (Barcelona)* [no. 1: 4] 1949.
"De unas declaraciones de Joan Miró, publicadas en 'La Publicitat' de Barcelona, el año 1928 . . . en 'Ahora' de Madrid, el año 1931."

2 [Statement]. *Variétés (Brussels)* p. XI June 1929.
Special surrealist number (hors-série). Also includes a "signed" declaration (bibl. 164).

3 [Statement]. *Minotaure* no. 3–4: 18 [Dec. 1933].
Included in bibl. 168.

4 Je rêve d'un grand atelier. *XXe Siècle* 1 no. 2: 25–28 May–June 1938.
Translated by J. J. Sweeney in Matisse Gallery catalogue, 1940 (bibl. 180); reprinted in San Francisco catalogue, 1948 (bibl. 186). German text in Scheidegger (bibl. 42).

5 [Enquête]. *Cahiers d'Art* no. 1–4: 73 1939.
Text in Duthuit's article (bibl. 135). Reprinted in Bille (bibl. 55), Guggenheim (bibl. 184), San Francisco (bibl. 186), Scheidegger (bibl. 42).

6 [Harlequin's Carnival]. *Verve* no. 4: 85 Jan.–Mar. 1939.
Comment on the painting, here reproduced in color. German text in Scheidegger (bibl. 42).

7 Jeux poétique. *Cahiers d'Art* 20–21: 269–272 1945–46.
Translated also in Platschek (bibl. 102) and Scheidegger (bibl. 42).

8 [Documents: statement]. *Transition Forty-Nine (Paris)* no. 5: 116 1949.

9 Minuscule. Texte et fac-similes de dessins de Miró. P. A. B., [Éditions P. A. Benoit, Alès]. 1954.

10 Ma dernière œuvre est un mur. *Derrière le Miroir* (Paris) no. 107–109: 24–25, 29 1958.
Translated in *Unesco Courrier* 11 no. 11: 34–36 Nov. 1958.

11 [Correspondence with Gérald Cramer]. 6 leaves, ports., 1947–1956.
Letters on their "A Toute Épreuve"; available in the Library of the Museum of Modern Art in photostatic copy.

Supplementary statements, quotations, brief extracts and the like are noted in bibl. 12–18, 32, 44, 89, 123, etc.

INTERVIEWS

12 BERNIER, ROSAMUND. Miro céramiste . . . une interview par correspondance . . . *L'Oeil* no. 17: 46, 49–53 ill. (col.) May 1956.
Also published, with variant texts and illustrations, in bibl. 108, 198. Abridged German versions in bibl. 42 and *Das Kunstwerk* 11 no. 12: 13 June 1958.

13 DUTHUIT, GEORGES. Où allez-vous Miró? *Cahiers d'Art* 11 no. 8–10: 261–262, 264 1936.
Partial translation in bibl. 42, 186.

14 J [ouffroy], A [lain]. Portrait d'un artiste: Joan Miró. *Arts (Paris)* no. 578: 8, July 25–31, 1956.

15 LEE, FRANCES. Interview with Miró. *Possibilities (N. Y.)* no. 1: 66–67 Winter 1947–48.

16 RODITI, EDOUARD. Interview with Joan Miró. *Arts (N. Y.)* 33 no. 1: 38–43 Oct. 1958.

17 SCHIFF, GERT. Joan Miró. *Das Kunstwerk* 7 no. 3–4: 66, 71 1953.
"Gespräche mit spanischen Malern: Dali–Joan Miró."

18 SWEENEY, JAMES J. Joan Miró: comment and interview. *Partisan Review* 15 no. 2: 206–212 Feb. 1948.
Also quoted in Allen Leepa, *The Challenge of Modern Art*, p. 190–194, New York, Beechhurst Press, 1949.

FILMS

19 MIRÓ. 1 reel (sound), 35 mm. Directed by Charles Estienne. [Paris, 1949.]

"Illustration et interprétation de la peinture de Joan Miró, à travers une série nombreuse de ses œuvres significatives." Reviewed: *Arts (Paris)*, July 1, 1949.

20 JOAN MIRÓ MAKES A COLOR PRINT. 2 reels (sound), 16 mm. (color). New York, Thomas Bouchard Productions, 1951. Commentary by S. W. Hayter and Ruthven Todd.

20a AROUND AND ABOUT JOAN MIRÓ. 16 mm. (sound), Kodachrome (1 hour). New York, Thomas Bouchard Productions [1956].

Begun 1947, includes work from 1915 to 1955. Also Spanish artistic traditions and locale. Camera: Bouchard et al. Sound: E. Varèse et al. Narrator: George Ross.

GRAPHIC WORKS

21 HIRTZ, LISE. "Il était une petite pie:" 7 chansons et 3 chansons pour Hyacinthe. 8 ill. (col.) Paris. Jeanne Bucher, 1928. Gouaches reproduced by pochoir. 300 copies in folio.

22 HUGNET, GEORGES. Enfances. 3 etchings Paris, Cahiers d'Art, 1935.

Printed by Lacourière (Paris) in edition of 100 copies.

23 TZARA, TRISTAN. Parler seul. 73 ill. (col.) Paris, Maeght, 1948–50.

Printed by Mourlot (Paris) in edition of 250 copies, with collage, color and black-and-white designs. Also his *L'Antitête, v. 3: Le Désespéranto* 8 etchings (Bordas, 1949).

24 DERRIÈRE LE MIROIR. No. 57–59 12 color lithographs Paris, Maeght, 1953.

Printed by Mourlot for the de luxe catalogues of the Maeght Gallery. Supplemented by graphics in nos. 14–15 (1948), 29–30 (1950), 87–89 (1956), 107–109 (1958). (See bibl. 96.)

25 CHAR, RENÉ. A la santé du serpent. Paris, G.L.M., 1954. Printed by Mourlot; 54 de luxe copies (1 color litho).

26 LEIRIS, MICHEL. Bagatelles végétales. 6 color etchings Paris, Jean Aubier, 1956.

Printed by Lacourière (Paris) in edition de luxe of 33 copies.

27 CHAR, RENÉ. Poem. Alès [Éditions P. A. Benoit], 1958. Two engravings on celluloid synthetic. Another celluloid print published by P. A. B. in his "Mon chemin" (1953).

28 CREVEL, RENÉ. La bague d'Aurore. 6 etchings (5 col.) Paris, Louis Broder, 1958.

Collection "Miroir du Poète", in an edition of 130 copies, supplemented by a portfolio of 22 etchings (75 copies).

29 ELUARD, PAUL. A toute épreuve. 80 color woodcuts Geneva, Gérald Cramer, 1958.

160 copies of "one of the most remarkable books of our time" (J.T.S.) Enric Tormo collaborated in the execution of the woodcuts. Technical details in bibl. 31, 36.

30 MIRÓ, JOAN. Constellations: album contenant 22 planches en couleurs. Texte inédit de André Breton. New York, Pierre Matisse, 1959.

Limited edition of 350 numbered and signed copies. Gouaches reproduced "en phototypie et au pochoir" by Jacomet.

BOOKS ON MIRO

31 [BERGGRUEN & CIE, Publisher.] Joan Miró: bois gravés pour un poème de Paul Eluard. 32 p. col. plates Paris, Berggruen, 1958.

Collection Berggruen, no. 25. Introduction by Douglas Cooper (2 p.). Booklet issued Apr. 1958 for the Galerie Berggruen's exhibition of "A Toute Épreuve" (published by Gérald Cramer). Also Berggruen plaquette no. 28: "Joan Miró, Constellations," 1959 (bibl. 30).

32 CIRICI-PELLICER, ALEJANDRO (?). Miró y la imaginación. 41 p. ill. (col.) Barcelona, Omega, 1949.

Quotes Miró. Footnotes.

33 CIRLOT, J. E. Joan Miró. 53 p. ill. (col.) Barcelona, Ediciones Cobalto, 1949.

Chronology of exhibitions and illustrative work.

34 ELGAR, FRANK. Miró. 8 p. plus 20 col. pl. Paris, Hazan [1954]. Booklet no. 30, Bibliothèque Aldine des Arts.

35 GREENBERG, CLEMENT. Joan Miró. 133 p. ill. New York, Quadrangle Press, 1948.

Bibliography by H. B. Muller, p. 123–127; illustrated books, p. 128. Also 1950 revised edition.

36 HUNTER, SAM. Joan Miró: his graphic work. XXXV plus 108 p. incl. ill. (col.) New York, Abrams, 1958.

Text (30 p.) plus footnotes. Select bibliography, p. 107–108, is largely list of illustrated books. "Copyright Hatje Verlag, Stuttgart, 1958."

37 HÜTTINGER, EDUARD. Miró. 31 p. plus 52 plates Berne, etc., Scherz, 1957.

38 LEIRIS, MICHEL. The prints of Joan Miró. 16 p. plus 50 plates (2 col.) New York, Curt Valentin, 1947.

Text also in French. Issued in small portfolio; de luxe edition includes original etchings.

39 MELO, JOAO CABRAL DE. Joan Miró. Barcelona, Ed. de l'Oc, 1950.
Edition of 125 copies "on pur fil guano" includes 3 color woodcuts.

40 PRÉVERT, JACQUES & RIBEMONT-DESSAIGNES, GEORGES. Joan Miró. 219 p. incl. ill. (col.) Paris, Maeght, 1956.
Poems by Prévert; text by Ribemont-Dessaignes (p. 69–95). Includes original lithographs, numerous illustrations, and bibliography (p. 217–219).

41 QUENEAU, RAYMOND. Joan Miró, ou Le poète préhistorique. 12 p. incl. 10 col. pl. Geneva, Skira, 1949.
Later issued in English series (Masterpieces of French painting) with 4 p. text.

42 SCHEIDEGGER, ERNST, ed. Joan Miró: Gesammelte Schriften, Fotos, Zeichnungen. 111 p. ill. (col.) Zurich, Arche, 1957.
Bilingual texts, including German translations, p. 7–32. Bibliography.

43 [SKIRA, Inc., Publisher]. Miró. 3 p. plus 6 col. plates. New York, Skira, 1955.
Introduction and commentaries unsigned. Skira color prints series (not bibl. 41).

44 SWEENEY, JAMES J. Joan Miro. 87 p. ill. New York, Museum of Modern Art, 1941.
Includes quotations from Miró (p. 13, 15, 32); bibliography (p. 85–87); chronology; list of works, catalogue of the museum's exhibition. Text partly reprinted in *Ars* (Mexico) May 1943.

45 SWEENEY, JAMES J. Joan Miró – Atmosphere. Preface by J. J. Sweeney. 105 p. incl. 93 ill. (5 col.) New York, Wittenborn, 1959.
"Intimate visit to the studio and surroundings in Barcelona."

46 VERDET, ANDRÉ. Joan Miró. 14 p. plus 25 ill. (col.) Nice, Galerie Matarasso, 1957.
Collection Sortilèges. Also de luxe edition: Sortilèges de Miró (1958).

47 VERDET, ANDRÉ & HAUERT, ROGER. Joan Miró. 32 p. ill. (ports.) Geneva, Kister, 1956.
"Les grands peintres"; images de Roger Hauert, biographical note; list of important works.

48 WEMBER, PAUL. Miró: das graphische Werk. [46 p.] ill. (col.) Krefeld, Kaiser Wilhelm Museum, 1957.
Catalogue of the "first total exhibition of the graphic work of Joan Miró." Text by Paul Wember. For details see bibl. 199.

GENERAL WORKS

49 Art Since 1945. p. 121–122, 164, 176, 240, 288, 294, ill. New York, Abrams, 1958.
Spain, by U. Apollonio, p. 121f.

50 Ballets Russes de Monte-Carlo. Programme. 1932.
Includes illustrations, color plates and data on "Jeux d'Enfants." Similar programs issued for subsequent and American performances (S. Hurok), etc.

51 BARR, ALFRED H., JR. Cubism and abstract art. p. 179–182, 217 ill. New York, Museum of Modern Art, 1936.
Also issued as exhibition catalogue. Miró, no. 170–174.

52 BARR, ALFRED H., JR. Fantastic art, dada, surrealism. 3. ed. 271 p. ill. New York, Museum of Modern Art, 1946.
Essay by Georges Hugnet. First ed. 1936 issued for museum's exhibition; second ed. 1937. Includes comprehensive text on the movement, important chronology, selected bibliography.

53 BARR, ALFRED H., JR. Masters of modern art. p. 142–143, 228 ill. (col.) New York, Museum of Modern Art, 1954.

54 BENET, RAFAEL. Historia de la pintura moderna, [v. 2]: Simbolismo. p. 12, 20, 188–189, 195, 197, 202 ill. Barcelona, Omega, 1953.

55 BILLE, EJLER. Picasso, surrealisme, abstrakt kunst. p. 149–168 ill. Copenhagen, Helios, 1945.
Miró texts, p. 167–168, from *Cahier d'Art* (1939).

56 BRETON, ANDRÉ. Entretiens, 1913–1952. p. 97, 134, 155, 162, 179, 221, 242–243 Paris, Gallimard, 1952.

57 BRETON, ANDRÉ. Les manifestes du surréalisme. p. 109 Paris, Le Sagittaire, 1955.
Miró noted in chronology on end-papers: 1924, 1925, 1928, 1930, 1931, 1933, 1937, 1941, 1949, 1952, 1954.

58 BRETON, ANDRÉ. Le surréalisme et la peinture. p. 62–65, plates 58–65 Paris, Gallimard, 1928.
Revised edition issued 1948.

59 BRETON, ANDRÉ. Le surréalisme et la peinture [etc.] p. 9, 68–70, 94 ill. New York, Brentano's, 1948.

60 BROCKWAY, WALLACE. The Albert D. Lasker collection: Renoir to Matisse. Commentaries by Wallace Brockway; introduction by Alfred Frankfurter. p. 101–102, 123 col. pl. New York, Simon and Schuster [1958].

61 BULLIET, C. J. The significant moderns. p. 107–110 ill. New York, Covici-Friede, 1936.

62 CIRICI-PELLICER, ALEJANDRO. El arte modernista catalán. p. 134, 306, 407, 424 Barcelona, Aymá, 1951.

63 [COBALTO, Publisher]. Surrealismo. p. 30, 32–34 ill. Barcelona, Cobalto, 1948.
"Cuaderno especial," v. 2, no. 1. Texts include essay by S. Gasch on Miró. Also note bibl. 117.

64 COGNIAT, RAYMOND. Histoire de la peinture. v. 2, p. 174, 290 col. pl. Paris, Nathan, 1955.

65 COURTHION, PIERRE. L'art indépendant: p. 152, 195–197, 266, 278, 292 ill. (col.) Paris, Michel, 1958.

66 DETAILLE, GEORGES & MULYS, GERARD. Les ballets de Monte-Carlo, 1911–1944. p. 118–121, 154–157 ill. Paris, Arc-en-Ciel, 1954.
On *Romeo and Juliet* and *Jeux d'Enfants*.

67 Dictionnaire Abrége du Surréalisme. 76 p. ill. p. 17; illus: p. 46, 48–49, 70 Paris, Galerie Beaux-Arts, 1938.
Also issued with catalogue insert: Exposition internationale du surréalisme, janvier-février 1938 (Galerie Beaux-Arts).

68 DORIVAL, BERNARD. Les étapes de la peinture contemporaine. v. 3, p. 210, 215, 222, 225, 228, 231, 287, 290. Paris, Gallimard, 1946.

69 DREIER, KATHERINE S. Modern art. p. 81 ill. (port.) New York, Société Anonyme – Museum of Modern Art, 1926.
Refers to Brooklyn Museum International for which a separate catalogue was issued.

70 DUTHUIT, GEORGES. Chinese mysticism and modern painting. p. 133–134 ill. Paris, Chroniques du Jour; London, Zwemmer, 1936.

71 EDWARDS, HUGH. Surrealism & its affinities; the Mary Reynolds Collection, a bibliography. Chicago, Art Institute of Chicago, 1956.
Note items 32, 50, 99, 147, 165, 208, 252, 290, 298, 318, 320, 346.

72 EINSTEIN, CARL. Die Kunst des 20. Jahrhunderts. 3. Aufl. p. 128, 428–433, 641 ill. Berlin, Propyläen, 1931.

73 ELUARD, PAUL. Voir. p. 56 col. pl. Geneva & Paris, Trois Collins, 1948.
Includes "Joan Miró" (poem) from *Capitale de la douleur* (Paris, Gallimard, 1928) and "Naissances de Miró" from *Donner à Voir* (Paris, Gallimard, 1939).

74 GAFFÉ, RENÉ. Introduction à la peinture française. p. 285–286 ill. Brussels, Éd. des Artistes, 1954.

75 GAFFÉ, RENÉ. Peinture à travers dada et le surréalisme. p. 49–57 ill. Brussels, Éd. des Artistes, 1952.

76 GASCOYNE, DAVID. A short survey of surrealism. p. 73, 75, 105, 107, 108, 133. London, Cobden-Sanderson, 1935.

77 GOLDWATER, ROBERT J. Primitivism in modern painting. p. 168–169 ill. New York & London, Harper, 1938.

78 GRIGSON, GEOFFREY. The arts today. p. 80–81, 88, 92–93, 96, 102–104, 106–108 ill. London, Lane, 1935.

79 GROHMANN, WILL. Bildende Kunst und Architektur. p. 193–197 et passim ill. Berlin, Suhrkamp, 1953.

80 GULLON, RICARDO. De Goya al arte abstracto. p. 113–141 ill. Madrid, Cultura Hispanica, 1952.

81 HAFTMANN, WERNER. Malerei im 20. Jahrhundert. v. 1, p. 402–408, 514 et passim; v. 2, p. 420–425 (ill.) Munich, Prestel, 1954–1955.

82 HESS, THOMAS B. Abstract painting. p. 61–63 ill. New York, Viking, 1951.

83 History of Modern Painting, [vol. 3]: From Picasso to Surrealism. p. 10, 11, 106, 150, 185–188, 200 col. pl. Geneva, Skira, 1950.
Texts by Raynal and others; biographical notes.

84 HITCHCOCK, HENRY-RUSSELL. Painting toward architecture. p. 41, 88, 89 ill. (col.) New York, Duell, Sloan and Pearce, 1948.
The Miller Company collection of abstract art.

85 HUNTER, SAM. Modern French painting, 1855–1956. p. 141–142 et passim. New York, Dell, 1956.

86 HUYGHE, RENÉ. French painting: The Contemporaries. p. 53–55, [175] pl. 140 New York, French and European, 1939.
Translated from the French edition.

87 HUYGHE, RENÉ, ed. Histoire de l'art contemporain. p. 317, 320, 325, 338–339, 341–342, 344, 363, 474, 492, 494, 516. Paris, Alcan, 1935.
Texts by Cassou, etc. and documentation by Bazin, originally issued in *L'Amour de l'Art (1934)*.

88 JAKOVSKI, ANATOLE. Six essais. p. 26–31 ill. Paris, Povolovsky [1933].

89 KATZENBACH AND WARREN, INC. Mural scrolls. Introduction by James T. Soby. 8 p. plus col. pl. [New York], Katzenbach & Warren, 1949.
Statements by the artists, p. [5], includes Miró.
KLINGEN 1942. See bibl. 158.

90 KOCHNO, BORIS. Le ballet . . . avec la collaboration de Maria Luz. p. 262–264, 266, 268, 287, 298, 304–307, 349, 363, 365 incl. ill. (col.) Paris, Hachette, 1954.

91 LAKE, CARLTON & MAILLARD, ROBERT. Dictionary of modern painting. p. 185–188 ill. (col.) New York, Paris Book Center [1955].
Translated from the French.

92 LASSAIGNE, JACQUES. Spanish painting from Velasquez to Picasso. p. 130–132, 139, 146. 3 col. pl. Geneva, Skira, 1952.
Other language editions.
LEEPA, ALLEN. The challenge of modern art. See bibl. 18.

93 LEVY, JULIEN. Surrealism. p. 19, 20, 148–149 ill. New York, Black Sun Press, 1936.

94 LOEB, PIERRE. Voyages à travers la peinture. p. 46–49, 82–83 ill. Paris, Bordas, 1946.

95 LOS ANGELES, UNIVERSITY OF CALIFORNIA. DEPARTMENT OF ART. Looking at modern painting. p. 50–52, 113 ill. (col.) Los Angeles, The University, 1957.
Surrealist chapter by F. S. Wight.

96 [MAEGHT, AIMÉ, Publisher.] 10 ans d'édition. p. 23–37, 47, incl. ill. (col.) Paris, Maeght, 1956.
Miró graveur, p. 23. Includes original print and list of graphic works. Special number of *Derrière le Miroir*. Oct. 1956. See also bibl. 118.

97 MARCHIORI, GIUSEPPE. Pittura moderna in Europa. p. 159–163 ill. Venice, Pozza, 1950.

98 MAYWALD, WILHELM. Portrait + Atelier. [part 12] ports. Zurich, Arche [1958].
"Miró" (8 p.) includes portraits, studio shots, a statement and one mss. letter. Additional photos published in Architecture d'Aujourd'hui's *Arts Plastiques*, 2. numéro hors série (1949) and as a separate: *Aristes chez Eux*, vus par Maywald.

99 MONRO, ISABEL S. & MONRO, KATE M. Index to reproductions of European paintings. p. 421. New York, Wilson, 1956.
References to a selected list of books and catalogue.

100 MUNSTERBERG, HUGO. Twentieth century painting. p. 67–69, 73 ill. New York, Philosophical Library, 1951.

101 NADEAU, MAURICE. Histoire du Surréalisme – Documents surréalistes. [376 p.] ill. Paris, Club des Éditeurs, 1958.
Biographical and bibliographical notes. Miró, p. 44. Revised edition: Paris, Éd. du Seuil, 1948.

102 PLATSCHEK, HANS, ed. Dichtung moderner Maler. p. 80, 83 ill. Wiesbaden, Limes, 1956.
Translates bibl. 7.

103 PLATTE, HANS. Malerei p. 272, 307 ill. Munich, Piper, 1957.

104 RAYNAL, MAURICE. Modern French painters. p. 126 ill. New York, Brentano, 1928.
Translation of "Anthologie de la peinture en France de 1906 à nos jours." p. 237–238 ill. Paris, Montaigne, 1927.

105 RAYNAL, MAURICE. Modern painting. p. 245–259, 310 et passim. ill. (col.) Geneva, Skira, 1953.
Other language editions. Also note bibl. 83.

106 READ, HERBERT, ed. Surrealism. Contributions by André Breton, Hugh Sykes Davies, Paul Eluard, Georges Hugnet. 251 p. ill. London, Faber & Faber, 1936.
Miró, pl. 54–57.

107 SCHMIDT, PAUL F. Geschichte der modernen Malerei. p. 256–257 col. pl. Zurich, Fretz & Wasmuth; Stuttgart, Kohlhammer, 1952.
Other editions, 1953, 1954, etc.

108 Selective Eye, 1956–1957. p. 6–13 ill. (col.) Paris & Lausanne, Bernier; New York, Reynal [1956].
Translated article from *L'Oeil* (bibl. 12).

109 SOBY, JAMES T. After Picasso. p. 49, 70, 90–91, 95–96, 99–101, 107–108 ill. Hartford, Mitchell; New York, Dodd, Mead, 1935.

110 SOBY, JAMES T. Contemporary painters. p. 99–103 ill. New York, Museum of Modern Art, 1948.
TAKIGUGHI. Album surréaliste. 1937. See bibl. 178.

111 THARRATS, JUAN-JOSÉ. Artistas españoles en el ballet. p. 29–33 ill. Barcelona, Buenos Aires, Argos, 1950.

112 VOLLMER, HANS. Allgemeines Lexikon der bildenden Künstler. v. 3, p. 399–400 Leipzig, Seemann, 1956.
Useful but incomplete bibliographical notes.

113 ZERVOS, CHRISTIAN. Histoire de l'art contemporain. p. 415 pl. 419–427 Paris, Cahiers d'Art, 1938.

SPECIAL NUMBERS

114 *L'Amic de les Arts.* no. 26 1928.
On Miró and surrealism, III no. 26: 198, 202–204 June 30, 1928. Texts by J. V. Foix, M. A. Cassanyes, Salvador Dali, S. Gasch, 7 illustrations, extracts from critiques on Bernheim Galerie show (George, Fierens, Tériade, etc.).

115 *Cahiers de Belgique.* no. 6 1929.
Special issue, 2 no. 6: 202–215 ill. June 1929, with texts by Sebastià Gasch, Robert Desnos, Salvador Dali, Waldemar George.

116 *Cahiers d'Arts.* no. 1–4 1934.
"L'Oeuvre de Joan Miró de 1917 à 1933," 9 no. 1–4: 11–58 (1934). Documentation, p. 54–55. Includes documentation, reviews and 2 color plates. Essays by Zervos, Raynal, Desnos, Péret, Hemingway, Gaffé, Hoppe, Antheil, Grohmann, Huidobro, Guéguen, Sweeney, Massine, Read, Foix, Viot, Jakovski. Also note bibl. 129.

117 *Cobalto (Barcelona).* no. 1 1949.
"Joan Miró," *Cobalto 49*, [no. 1]: 1–8 ill. (col., port.) [1949]. Includes "Miró y los criticos," "Declaraciones de Joan Miró," "Miró y los poetas," "Miró y sus amigos," catalogue of Galerias Layetans show, Apr. 23–May 6 (reviewed by C. in no. 2).

118 *Derrière le Miroir.* no. 14–15; 29–30; 57–59; 87–89; special number Oct. 1956; 107–109 1948–1958.
De luxe periodical and catalogue of the Galerie Maeght, Paris, with numerous illustrations and color plates. No. 14–15 (Nov.–Dec. 1948) includes texts by Tzara, Cassou, Prats-Valles, Queneau, Duthuit, Zervos, Limbour, Gomis, Eluard, Kahnweiler, Deharme, Raynal, Loeb, Artigas; also list of exhibited works. No. 29–30 (May–June 1950) includes list of works, texts by Leiris, Queneau, Prévert. No. 57–59 (June–Aug. 1953) lists 100 works, with 17 pages of original lithos executed for the 60th anniversary show. No. 87–89 (June–Aug. 1956) is titled "Miró-Artigas," lists 43 works, and includes texts by Artigas, Prévert and Ribemont-Dessaignes (from bibl. 40). A special number (Oct. 1956) reports Maeght's graphic production: 10 Ans d'Édition (bibl. 96). No. 107–109 (1958) lists exhibited works, including the Unesco wall decoration and text (bibl. 10).

119 *Gaceta de Arte.* no. 38 1936.
No. 38: 5–22 ill. (June 1936) includes main essay by E. Westerdahl, texts by Hoppe, Huidobro, Massine, Zervos. Documentation, p. 21–22.

120 *Mizué (Tokio).* no. 570 1953.
No. 570: 1–48 ill. (col. pl.) Feb. 1953. Includes Japanese text of essay by Georges Duthuit, supplementary text and plates (including Miró cover). Additional data in *Mizué* no. 620: 3–22 ill. (col.) Mar. 1957 (article by I. Yanihara on Miró's ceramics). For special 1937 number *Album surréaliste* issued as exhibition catalogue, see bibl. 178.

ARTICLES

121 AGUELAR, MANUEL. Ode de poche pour Joan Miró. *Cahiers du Sud* 33 no. 280: 388–390 1946.

122 ARAGON, LOUIS & BRETON, ANDRÉ. Protestation. *La Revolution Surréaliste* 2 no. 7: 31. Also a separate: June 15, 1926. "Contre la participation de Miró et de Max Ernst au spectacle des ballets russes." Reprinted bibl. 101.

123 ASHTON, DORE. Miró – Artigas. *Craft Horizons* 17 no. 1: 16–20 ill. Feb. 1957.
Includes Miró statements.

124 BATAILLE, GEORGES. Joan Miró: peintures récentes. *Documents* 2 no. 7: 398–403 incl. ill. 1930.

125 BERNIER, ROSAMUND. Miro céramiste. *L'Oeil* no. 17 1956. See bibl. 12.

126 BLOCK, MAXINE, ed. Miró. *Current Biography* May 1940.
Also published in the Current Biography Yearbook 1940, p. 587–589.

127 BOSSCHÈRE, JEAN DE. Notes sur la peinture et Miró. *Variétés (Brussels)* 1: 132–139 July 15, 1928.

128 BRETON, ANDRÉ. Constellations de Joan Miró. *L'Oeil* no. 48: 50–55 incl. ill. (col.) Dec. 1958.
Text also published in Matisse edition (bibl. 30).

129 CAHIERS D'ART. Edited by Christian Zervos. Paris, 1929 – current.
Outstanding coverage on Miró, including not only the special study (bibl. 116) but numerous articles, poems, reviews and illustrations, e. g. p. 359 ff. (1929); p. 69 ff. (1930); p. 61 ff., p. 335 ff., p. 424 ff. (1931); p. 115 ff. (1935); p. 257 ff. (1936); p. 76 ff. (1937); p. 37 ff. (1940); p. 273 ff. (1945–46); p. 293 (1947); p. 32 ff. (1952); p. 273 (1953). Also note bibl. 151, 167, 170, 174, etc.

130 CASSANYES, M. A. Joan Miró, el extraordinario. *A. C. (Barcelona)* no. 18: 40–41 ill. 1935.

131 CLARK, ELIOT. Milestones in modern art: 'Catalan Landscape (The Hunter)' by Joan Miro. *Studio* 154 no. 774: 84–85 col. pl. Sept. 1957.

COOPER, DOUGLAS. [Joan Miró]. 1958. See bibl. 31.
A revealing introduction to the Collection Berggruen booklet.

132 COURTHION, PIERRE. Jeux et fantasie de Miró. *XXe Siècle* (n. s.) no. 6: 40–44 incl. ill. (col.) Jan. 1956.
In special number on "le papier collé."

133 DORFLES, GILLO. Per Joan Miró. *Critica d'Arte* 8: 332–334 ill. Nov. 1949.

134 DUPIN, JACQUES. Miró. *Quadrum* no. 1: 95–106 ill. (col.) May 1956.
English summary, p. 222.

135 DUTHUIT, GEORGES. Enquête. *Cahiers d'Art* 14 no. 1–4: 65, 73 ill. 1939.

136 DUTHUIT, GEORGES. Fantasy in Catalonia. *Magazine of Art* 30: 440–443, 462 ill. July 1937.

DUTHUIT, GEORGES. Où allez-vous, Miró? *Cahiers d'Art.* See bibl. 13.

DUTHUIT. [Miró] Mizué. See bibl. 120.

137 ESTIENNE, CHARLES. Poésie des formes et des couleurs. *XXe Siècle* no. 1: 31–38 incl. ill. (col.) June 8, 1951.

138 FREY, JOHN C. Miró and the Surrealists. *Parnassus* 8 no. 5: 13–15 ill. Oct. 1936.

FITZSIMMONS, JAMES. On the "peintures sauvages" of Joan Miró. See bibl. 203.

139 GASCH, SEBASTIÀ. L'obra del pintor Joan Miró. *L'Amic de les Arts* 1 no. 5: 15–17 ill. Aug. 1926.
Also no. 7 (Oct. 1926); no. 20: 108 Nov. 1927.

140 GASCH, SEBASTIÀ. Joan Miró. *Das Kunstwerk* 4 no. 5: 21–25 ill. (col.) 1950.
Also note bibl. 63.

141 GASSIER, PIERRE. Miró et Artigas. *Labyrinthe* 2 no. 22–23: 10–11 ill. Dec. 1946.

142 GAYA NUÑO, J. A. Medio siglo de movimiento vanguardistas en nuestra pintura. *Dau al Set (Barcelona)* p. [10, 11, 18] Dec. 1950.

143 GEORGE, WALDEMAR. Miro et le miracle ressuscité. *Centaure* 3: 201–204 ill. 1929.
Illustrations, p. 200, 205, 219.

144 GOMEZ SICRE, JOSÉ. Joan Miro in New York. *Right Angle (Washington D.C.)* 1 no. 10: [5–6] ill. Jan. 1948.

145 GUÉGUEN, PIERRE. L'humour féerique de Joan Miró. *XXe Siècle* no. 8: 39–44 incl. ill. (col.) Jan. 1957.

146 GUSMÃO, ADRIANO DE. A cerâmica de Joan Miró. *Arquitectura Portuguesa Cerâmica e Edifiçacão Reunidas (Lisbon)* p. 6–10 ill. 1948.

147 ELUARD, PAUL. Naissances de Miró. *Cahiers d'Art* 12 no.1–3: 78–80 ill. 1937.
Reprinted in bibl. 73.

148 HUGNET, GEORGES. Joan Miró; ou L'enfance de l'art. *Cahiers d'Art* 6 no. 7–8: 335–40 ill. 1931.
Also poem, 15 no. 3–4: 48 1940.

149 HUGNET, GEORGES. Peinture poésie. *Pagany (Boston)* 1 no. 2: 107 Spring 1930.

150 JACOB, MAX. Una carta inédita de Max Jacob a Joan Miró [29. mai 1922]. *Cobalto 49 (Barcelona)* no. 3: 3 1950.

151 LARREA, JUAN. Miroir d'Espagne. *Cahiers d'Art* 12 no. 4–5: 157–159 ill. 1937.
"À propos du 'Faucheur' de Miró, au pavillon espagnol de l'exposition 1937."

152 LEIRIS, MICHEL. Joan Miró. *Documents* 1 no. 5: 263–269 ill. Oct. 1929.

153 LEIRIS, MICHEL. Joan Miró. *Little Review (New York)* p. 8–9 ill. Spring-Summer 1926.

154 LIMBOUR, GEORGES. Souvenirs sur un peintre, Joan Miró. *Arts de France* no. 17–18: 47, 49–50 ill. 1947.

155 LIMBOUR, GEORGES. Un nouveau Miró. *XXe Siècle* no. 7: 16–20 incl. ill. June 1956.

156 Miro vous montre Barcelona. *L'Oeil* no. 7–8: 52–59 ill. (port.) Summer 1955.

157 MORRIS, GEORGE L. K. Miró and the Spanish Civil war. *Partisan Review* 4 no. 3: 32–33 ill. Feb. 1938.

158 MORTENSEN, RICHARD. Joan Miró. p. 75–78 ill. IN KLINGEN 1942. Copenhagen, Fischer [1942].

159 La Révolution Surréaliste. Paris, 1925–1929.
In addition to Aragon (bibl. 122), references include no. 4: 5, 15 ill. July 15, 1925; no. 5: 25 ill. Oct. 15, 1925; no. 7: 19 ill. Dec. 1926; no. 9–10: 62 ill. Oct. 1, 1927; no. 11: [II] Mar. 15, 1928; no. 12: 52 Nov. 15, 1929.

160 ROH, FRANZ. Miró als Keramiker. *Kunstwerk* 11 no. 12: 3–4 ill. (col.) plates (p. 5–12); also cover.

161 SANTOS, TORROELLA, R. Joan Miró en su estudio. *Indice de las Artes (Madrid)* p. 3 ill. Feb. 1950.

161a SCHNEIDER, PIERRE. Miró. *Horizon* 1 no. 4: 70–81 incl. ill. (port.), col. plates Mar. 1959.
Color plate on cover.

162 SINDREU, CARLES. Joan Miró. *D'Aci i d'Alla (Barcelona)* 22 no. 79: 56 ill. 1934.
Includes original pochoir in color.

163 STAHLY, F. A surrealist mural in an American hotel. *Graphis* 4 no. 22: 147, 194 ill. 1948.
Also see "Mural in Cincinnati's Terrace Plaza hotel" *Architectural Forum* 88: 148 ill. 1948.

164 Le surréalisme en 1929. *Variétés (Brussels)* no. hors série June 1929.
Includes "A suivre... Paris 1929," manifesto "signed" by Miró, among others, and a statement.

165 SWEENEY, JAMES J. Miro. *Art News* 52 no. 7, part 2: 58–81, 185–188 ill. (col.) Nov. 1953.

> The Art News Annual XXIII (1954), with special gouache in color, quotations, etc. Additional commentary on Miró may be found in *Theatre Arts* 33 no. 2: 38–41 ill. Mar. 1949.

166 SWEENEY, JAMES J. [Preface to Miró exhibition catalogue]. New York, Pierre Matisse Gallery, 1953.

> Important text in bibl. 192, with Miró quotations.

167 TÉRIADE, E. Documentation sur la jeune peinture. *Cahiers d'Art* 5 no. 2: 76, 84 ill. 1930.

168 TÉRIADE, E. Émancipation de la peinture. *Minotaure* no. 3–4: 9–20 ill. 1934.

> Includes Miró statement, p. 18. Also "La peinture surréaliste," no. 8: 5, 16 ill. June 15, 1936.

169 TZARA, TRISTAN. À propos de Joan Miró. *Cahiers d'Art* 15 no. 3–4: 37–47 incl. ill. 1940.

> Additional commentary in "Le papier collé," 6 no. 2: 64–74 1931; "Pour passer le temps," no. 20–21: 277–292 1946.

170 VIOT, JACQUES. Un ami, Joan Miró. *Cahiers d'Art* 11 no. 8–10: 257–60 1936.

> Plates, p. 258–260.

171 WATSON, PETER. Joan Miró. *Horizon* 4 no. 20: 131–133 ill. 1941.

172 WEISS, HUGH. Miró – magic with rocks. *Art News* 55 no. 4: 48–49, 56–58 incl. ill. Summer 1956.

> Photos by Sabine Weiss.

173 WESCHER, HERTA. Collages dadaistes et surréalistes. *Art d'Aujourd'hui* 5 no. 2–3: 17–20 ill. Mar.–Apr. 1954.

174 ZERVOS, CHRISTIAN. Remarques sur les œuvres récentes de Miró. *Cahiers d'Art* 24 no. 1: 115–137 incl. ill. (col.) 1949.

> Also numerous references, e.g. "La nouvelle génération," no. 9–10: 379 1926, no. 9–10: 424–426 1931, and material edited by Zervos, e.g. bibl. 116, 129.

SELECTED CATALOGUES (By date)

175 LA LICORNE, GALERIE. Exposition de peintures et dessins de Joan Miró de 29 avril au 14 mai. Catalogue illustré. Texte de Maurice Raynal. 12 p. incl. ill. Paris, 1921.

> 29 works, 15 drawings, 4 illustrations. Preface reprinted bibl. 116.

176 GOEMANS, GALERIE. Exposition de collages . . . La peinture au défi, par Aragon. p. 19, 26–29, 31–32 ill. Paris, 1930.

> March exhibit; nos. 22–24 by Miró; 2 illustrations.

177 NEW BURLINGTON GALLERIES. The international surrealist exhibition. 32 p. London, 1936.

> No. 208–229 by Miró, plus objects. Held June 11–July 4 (over 400 exhibits). Preface by A. Breton and H. Read.

178 MIZUÉ (Periodical). Album surréaliste, ed. by Shuzo Takiguchi & Tiroux Yamanaka. Tokio, 1937.

> Major Japanese international at the Nippon Salon with oriental text and some English captions. Nos. 81–87 by Miró, 7 illustrations.

179 MAYOR GALLERY. Joan Miró exhibition. London, [London, Bulletin], 1938.

> Catalogue issued in the *London Bulletin* no. 2: 3–5 ill. May 1938. Lists 19 works; poem by R. Todd; note by D. Lord, p. 20.

180 MATISSE, PIERRE, GALLERY. Joan Miró: exhibition of early paintings from 1918 to 1925. [20 p.] incl. 12 ill. New York, Mar. 1940.

> Includes "I dream of a large studio" (bibl. 4). 14 works shown Mar. 12–31.

181 GALLATIN, A. E., COLLECTION. Museum of living art, A. E. Gallatin collection. p. 11, 33–34 ill. New York, 1940.

> Includes 6 works; notes by G. L. K. Morris; preface by Hélion. Other catalogues: Gallery of Living Art, N.Y.U., 1930. – Gallery of Living Art, N.Y.U., 1933. – Museum of Living Art, N.Y.U., 1933. – Museum of Living Art, N.Y.U., 1936. Also 1954 edition bibl. 193.

182 NEW YORK. MUSEUM OF MODERN ART. Joan Miro, by James Johnson Sweeney. 87 p. ill. 1941.

> Issued with catalogue of exhibition, Nov. 18, 1941–Jan. 11, 1942. List of works, p. 81–84. See bibl. 44.

183 CHRYSLER, WALTER P., JR. Collection of Walter P. Chrysler, Jr. exhibition. p. 15–16, 77–80 ill. Richmond, Va., Virginia Museum of Fine Arts, 1941.

> Also exhibited Philadelphia Museum of Art. No. 137–148 by Miró. Preface by H. McBride.

184 GUGGENHEIM, PEGGY, ed. Art of This Century. p. 22, 112–114 incl. ill. New York, Art of This Century, 1942.

> Lists 3 works, text by Breton, quotations from Miró (Cahiers d'Art, 1939).

185 Le Surréalisme en 1947. Exposition internationale du surréalisme, présentée par André Breton et Marcel Duchamp. p. 86, 134 pl. VII Paris, Maeght, 1947.

> Edition de luxe included original Miró litho. Colophon: finished June 27, 1947.

186 SAN FRANCISCO, MUSEUM OF ART. Picasso, Gris, Miró: the Spanish masters of twentieth century painting, p. 11, 38–39, 42–45, 89–107 ill. San Francisco, 1948.

Also exhibited at the Portland Art Museum. Texts by J. Larrea, Man Ray, H. Read, "From the artist himself," p. 94–96 includes translations from *Cahiers d'Art* (1936 and 1939) *XXe Siècle* (1938). Plates 97–107.

187 NEW YORK, MUSEUM OF MODERN ART. Painting and sculpture in the Museum of Modern Art, ed. by Alfred H. Barr, Jr. p. 126, 215–218, 278, 315 New York, 1948.

11 works, and illustrations. Later additions reported in museum's bulletins: 20 no. 3–4: 45 1953; 23 no. 3: 37 1956.

188 BERN. KUNSTHALLE. Joan Miro, Margrit Linck, Oskar Dalvit. p. 1–13, 8 ill. Bern, 1949.

94 works shown Apr. 21–May 29. Foreword, catalogue, extensive bibliography.

189 CHICAGO. ART INSTITUTE. 20th century art from the Louise and Walter Arensberg collection. p. 6, 8, 30–31 2 ill. Chicago, 1949.

Shown Oct. 20–Dec. 18. New catalogue issued when the collection was acquired by Philadelphia: The Louise and Walter Arensberg collection. p. [16], plates 144–152 Philadelphia, Museum of Art, 1954.

190 LONDON. INSTITUTE OF CONTEMPORARY ART. 40,000 years of modern art, by W. G. Archer & Robert Melville. p. 39–43 ill. London, 1949.

No. 148–152 by Miró.

191 YALE UNIVERSITY. ART GALLERY. Collection of the Société Anonyme. p. 108–109 ill. New Haven, Conn., Associates in Fine Arts, Yale University, 1950.

Text by M. Duchamp, K. S. Dreier; documentation.

192 MATISSE, PIERRE, GALLERY. Miró, recent paintings. 24 p. ill. New York, 1953.

Text by J. J. Sweeney. 60th Anniversary exhibit, listing 63 works shown Nov. 17–Dec. 12. Original color lithographs; also limited edition.

193 GALLATIN, A. E. COLLECTION. A. E. Gallatin collection – "Museum of Living Art." p. 17, 44, 60, 114, 115, 151 ill. (col., port.) Philadelphia, Museum of Art, 1954.

No. 118–123 by Miró. Also earlier catalogues (bibl. 181).

194 KREFELD. KAISER WILHELM MUSEUM. Miró 1954. [18] p. incl. ill. (col.) Krefeld, 1954.

Text by P. Wember and W. Grohmann. Catalogue of exhibit also shown at Stuttgart (Württembergische Staatsgalerie).

195 BRUSSELS. PALAIS DES BEAUX-ARTS. Joan Miró. [48] p. ill. (col.) Brussels, 1956.

144 works exhibited Jan. 6–Feb. 7. Texts from *Derrière le Miroir* (bibl. 118). Another catalogue, bibl. 196.

196 BRUSSELS. PALAIS DES BEAUX-ARTS. Joan Miró. [48] p. ill. (col.) Brussels, Connaissance, 1956.

Text in Dutch and French. Exhibit held Jan.–Feb. at Brussels and Feb.–Mar. at Amsterdam (Stedelijk Museum). Texts extracted from previously published writings.

197 MAEGHT, AIMÉ, GALERIE. Miró-Artigas: Terres de grand feu. Paris, 1956.

Issued in typical gallery format, as no. 87–89 of *Derrière le Miroir*, June–Aug. Lists 34 works. For other catalogues in similar format see bibl. 118.

198 MATISSE, PIERRE, GALLERY. Sculpture in ceramic by Miró and Artigas. 20 p. ill. (col.) New York, 1956.

24 works shown December. Reprints Bernier's "Miró the ceramist" (bibl. 108). Cover and insert are original lithographs.

199 KREFELD. KAISER WILHELM MUSEUM. Miró, das graphische Werk. [46] p. ill. (col.) Krefeld, 1957.

Multilingual catalogue of the "first total exhibition of the Graphic Work of Joan Miró." Text by Paul Wember. Exhibited April 1957; later at Berlin, Munich, Cologne, Hanover and Hamburg.

200 HANOVER. KESTNER GESELLSCHAFT. Joan Miró, das graphische Gesamtwerk. 30 p. ill. Hanover, 1957.

The Krefeld circulating exhibit (bibl. 199) reported in the format of the typical Kestner catalogue. Exhibited Dec. 11, 1957–Jan. 19, 1958.

201 PULITZER, LOUISE & PULITZER, JOSEPH, JR., COLLECTION. Modern painting, drawing & sculpture. 2 v. ill. Cambridge, Harvard College, 1957.

Vol. 1, p. 59–60 (text by J. Pulitzer, Jr.). Catalogue of exhibit at Knoedler & Co., N.Y., and the Fogg Art Museum. – Vol. 2, p. 234–235. Catalogue by C. S. Chetham.

202 LIÈGE. MUSÉE DE L'ART WALLOON. Léger – Matisse – Picasso – Miro – Laurens – Magnelli – Arp – Hartung – Jacobsen. p. 109–130 incl. ill. Liège, 1958.

Catalogue of 40 works; exhibited July–Sept. 1958, "Musée de l'Art Walloon." Text by J. Dupin (3 p.); documentation.

203 MATISSE, PIERRE, GALLERY. Miró – "peintures sauvages" 1934 to 1953. Introduction by James Fitzsimmons. 32 p. 21 ill. New York, 1958.

Catalogue of 21 works exhibited Nov. 4–29. Extensive text.

INDEX

Page numbers marked with an asterisk denote illustrations

Alsdorf, Mr. and Mrs. James W., collection, see *View of a Farm; View of Montroig*

Altamira wall paintings, 140

"*Amour*," *48

Aragon, Louis, 60, 149

Arp, Jean (Hans), 62, 66; *Madame Torso with Wavy Hat*, 66, *150

Artigas, José Lloréns, 8, 110–111, 117–118, 135, 137, 138, 140, 147; works (with Miró), see *Ceramic; Day; Head* (Matisse Gallery); *Head* (Osborn); *Night* (mural); *Personage* (ceramic); *Portico; Vase*

Art nouveau, 58, 62

Ault, Mr. and Mrs. Lee A., collection, see *Figures and Mountains*

Awakening at Dawn, *104, 106

La Bague d'Aurore, 135

Ballet, designs for, 66, 70; see also *Jeux d'Enfants; Roméo et Juliette*

A Ballet Dancer Listening to Organ Music in a Gothic Cathedral, *113, 118

Baltimore Museum of Art, see *Persons Attracted by the Form of the Mountain; Portrait I; Woman and Bird under the Moon*

Barcelona, 7, 8, 14, 19, 32, 58, 70, 80, 100, 106, 140; Academy Galí, 9–10, 12; St. Luke Academy, 110; School of Fine Arts, 8, 9, 10

Barr, Alfred H., Jr., 37, 70, 149

Bartos, Mr. and Mrs. Armand P., collection, see *The Harbor*

The Beautiful Bird Revealing the Unknown to a Pair of Lovers, *105, 106

Bird (bronze), *110

Birds, Figures, and Blue Star, 130, *132

Block, Mr. and Mrs. Leigh B., collection, see *The Olive Grove*

Böcklin, Arnold, 8, 9

Book illustrations, see *La Bague d'Aurore; A Toute Epreuve*

Bosch, Hieronymus, 36

Bouchard, Thomas, 138

Bragaline, Edward A., see *The Chauffeur*

Breton, André, 39, 45, 60, 106, 149, 150; *Manifeste du surréalisme*, 38, 149; *Poisson soluble*, 38; *La révolution surréaliste*, 38; *Le surréalisme et la peinture*, 60, 149

Broder, Louis, 135

Buffalo, Albright Art Gallery, see *The Harlequin's Carnival; Woman and Bird in the Night*

Bunshaft, Mr. and Mrs. Gordon, collection, see *Painting*

Cambridge, Mass., Fogg Art Museum, see Mural in Harkness Commons, study for

Cambridge, Mass., Harvard University, see Mural in Harkness Commons

The Candle, *47, 48

Catalonia, Catalan, 7, 8, 14, 28, 38, 53, 58, 66, 88, 118, 123

Catalan Landscape (The Hunter), 37–38, *39, 45

Catalan Peasant, *42

Ceramic, *111

Ceramics, 8, 110–*111, 117–118, *134, *135, *136, *137, 138, 140, *146, 147

Cézanne, Paul, 12, 14

The Chauffeur, 14, *17

Chicago, Art Institute, see *Woman and Birds in front of the Sun*

de Chirico, Giorgio, 45

Cincinnati, Terrace Hilton Hotel, see *Mural*

Clifford, Mr. and Mrs. Henry, collection, see *The Tilled Field*

The Coffee Pot, *11

Coiffeur Disheveled by the Flight of Constellations, 138, *143

Colin, Mr. and Mrs. Ralph F., collection, see *Awakening at Dawn; The Poetess*

Collage, 7, *15, 60, *61, 70, *74, *75, *133, 149

Collage (Matisse Gallery), *75; *Collage* (Neumann), *75; *Collage* (Miró), 70, *149; *Collage* ("*Le Papillon*"), *74; *Collage* (Private collection, New York), *74

Composition (Maeght), 130, *133

Composition (1933, Museum of Modern Art), see *Painting* (Museum of Modern Art)

Composition (1933, Wadsworth Atheneum), see *Painting* (Wadsworth Atheneum)

Composition (Werner), 66, *68

"Constellations," 100, *104, *105, 106, *107, 130

Construction, *64, 66

Copley, Mr. and Mrs. William N., collection, see "*Objet*"

"*Le corps de ma brune ...*," *46, 48

Cramer, Gérald, 137, 138, 150; collection, see *Jeux d'Enfants*, designs for

Crevel, René, 60

Cubism and cubist, 14, 23, 24, 26, 28, 98

Cuttoli, Mme Marie, collection, see "*Le corps de ma brune ...*"

Dada and dadaist, 23, 24, 38

Dalmau, José, 14, 19

Day, 138, 140, 147

Deutsch, Mr. and Mrs. Richard, collection, see *Birds, Figures, and Blue Star*

Diaghilev, 19, 66

Dog Barking at the Moon, *53

A Drop of Dew Falling from the Wing of a Bird Awakening Rosalie Asleep in the Shadow of a Cobweb, *102

Duchamp, Mrs. Marcel, collection, see *The Farmer's Wife*

Dufy, Raoul, 110

Dutch Interior (Guggenheim), *54

Dutch Interior (Marx), *56, 58

Dutch Interior (Museum of Modern Art), *57, 58

Dutch Interiors, 45, 55–58, 60

Dutch Little Masters, 55, 58

The Ear of Grain, *34

Eluard, Paul, 60, 138, 139; see also *A Toute Epreuve*

Emery's Sons, Thomas, Inc., collection, see *Mural* (Cincinnati)

Engleheart, George, *Portrait of Mrs. Mills*, 60, *62

Ernst, Max, 66, 70, 74

The Family, *38, 39
The Farm, 14, 32, *33, 34, 36, 45
The Farmer's Wife, 34, *35
Fauves and fauvism, 12, 14, 23
de Fernández, Mme Dolores Miró, collection, see *The Village of Montroig*
Figure, *79
Figures and Mountains, 80, *86
Flemish painters, 36, 80
"La Fornarina," 60, *65
Fratellini, *51, 53
Frélaut, Jacques, 150
Friedman, Mr. and Mrs. B. H., collection, see *Collage ("Le Papillon")*

Gaffé, René, 48, 149
Galí, Francisco de Asís, 10
Gassier, Pierre, 111, 150
Gaudí, Antoni, 58; Park Güell, 140
Gauguin, Paul, 137
Glove and Newspaper, see *Table with Glove*
van Gogh, Vincent, 12, 14, 24
Goodyear, Mrs. A. Conger, see *Figure*
Greenberg, Clement, 58, 99, 149, 150
Gris, Juan, 7, 32, 66
Guggenheim, Peggy, see *Dutch Interior*

The Harbor, *115, 118
The Harlequin's Carnival, *44, 45
Hartford, Wadsworth Atheneum, see *Painting*
Harvard mural, see Mural in Harkness Commons
Head (ceramic, Matisse Gallery), *137
Head (ceramic, Osborn), *135
Head of a Man, 80, *82
Head of a Peasant, *43
Head of a Woman, 98, *101
Help Spain (Aidez Espagne), *91
Hemingway, Ernest, 32, 149; see *The Farm*
Herrera, Jaime, 150
"L'hirondelle d'amour," 74, *81
Holland, 45, 53, 55, 58
Holty, Carl, 122, 123
Hope Returns to Us through the Flight of Constellations, 138, *145
Hugnet, Georges, 28, 32, 149

Iowa City, University of Iowa, see *A Drop of Dew* ...

Jarry, Alfred, *Ubu Roi*, 45
Jeux d'Enfants, designs for, 66, *71

Kansas City, Nelson Gallery—Atkins Museum, see *Women at Sunrise*
Kitchen Garden with Donkey, 14, 19, *21
Klee, Paul, 60

Landscape, 39, *40
Larrea, Juan, 88, 150
Laughlin, Mrs. James, collection, see *Women by the Lake* ...
Lévy, M. and Mme Raoul, collection, see *Coiffeur Disheveled* ...
Loeb, Pierre, 80; see Paris, Galerie Pierre

Maitland, Dr. and Mrs. Leslie M., collection, see *Vase of Flowers and Butterfly*
Makepeace, Mr. and Mrs. Le Roy, collection, see *The Night*
Mallorca, 8, 100, 106
Man with a Pipe, 45, *50
Man, Woman, and Child, 66, *67
Marcoussis, Louis, 93
Marx, Mr. and Mrs. Samuel A., collection, see *Dutch Interior; Portrait of E. C. Ricart*
Massine, Léonide, 66
Maternity, 39, *41
Matisse, Henri, 7, 26, 28, 60; *The Red Studio*, *19, 28
Matisse, Pierre, 93, 98; see also New York, Pierre Matisse Gallery
Matisse, Mr. and Mrs. Pierre, collection, see "Objet poétique"; Painting; Seated Nude
Miller, Mr. and Mrs. C. Earle, collection, see *Still Life with Toy Horse*
Minneapolis Institute of Arts, see *The Family*
Miró, Joan, photographs of, *frontispiece, *134; film on, 138
Montroig, 7, 32, 80, 110, 137
The Moon, *124, 127
Mural in Harkness Commons, 91, 122–124, 126–127, *130–131; study for, 123–124, 126, *131
Mural (Cincinnati, Terrace Hilton Hotel), 91, 120, *122–123, 124, 127, 137, 150
Murals, 91; see also *Day; Mural* (Cincinnati); Mural in Harkness Commons; *Night; Nursery Decoration; The Reaper*

Naville, Pierre, *La révolution surréaliste*, 38
Neumann, Mr. and Mrs. Morton G., collection, see *Collage; Painting; Spanish Dancer*
New York, The Solomon R. Guggenheim Museum, see *Painting; Portico*
New York, Pierre Matisse Gallery, 100; see also *Ceramic; Collage; Head* (ceramic); *Painting-poem; Personage* (ceramic); *Personage in the Night; Two Personages in Love with a Woman; Vase; View of Montroig*
New York, Museum of Modern Art, 122; see also *The Beautiful Bird* ...; *Catalan Landscape; Construction; Dutch Interior; The Ear of Grain; Help Spain; Painting; Rope and People; Table with Glove; A Toute Epreuve*
New York, Stanhope Hotel, see *Women Listening to Music*
Night (mural), 138, 140, *146, 147
The Night, 120, *121
Nocturne (Private collection, New York), *96
Nocturne (Penrose), *84
Noyes, Mr. and Mrs. Eliot, see *Bird*
Nude, *52, 53
Nursery Decoration, 91, *98–99

"Objet," *77
"Objet poétique," *77, 80
The Olive Grove, *23, 28
Onstad, Mr. and Mrs. Niels, collection, see *Women in the Night*
Oriental art, 118, 138
Osborn, Mr. and Mrs. Robert, collection, see *Head* (ceramic)

Painting (Bunshaft), *128, 130; *Painting* (Guggenheim), 138, *140; *Painting* (Matisse), 48, *49; *Painting* (Museum of Modern Art), 70, *73; *Painting* (Neumann), *127; *Painting* (Thompson), 138, *142; *Painting* (Wadsworth Atheneum), 70, *72; *Painting* (Weil), 138, *141
Painting-poem, 96, *97
Paris, 7, 8, 10, 19, 23, 24, 28, 32, 39, 53, 55, 58, 80, 83, 100, 138, 147
Paris, Doucet Foundation, see *Landscape*
Paris, Galerie La Licorne, 19, 53
Paris, Galerie Maeght, 123; see also *The Coffee Pot; Composition; Hope Returns* ...; *The Peasant; The Red Disk* ...; *Woman*

Paris, Galerie Pierre, 80
Paris, UNESCO, see *Day; Night* (mural)
Paris Exposition of 1937, Spanish Pavilion, 88, 91
Pascó, José, 9, 10
The Peasant, *10
Penrose, Roland, collection, see *Catalan Peasant; Maternity; Nocturne*
Péret, Benjamin, *La révolution surréaliste*, 38
Person in the Presence of Nature, 74, 80, *83
Personage (ceramic), 130, *135
Personage and Moon, *129, 130
Personage in the Night (Matisse), 106, *108
Personages in the Night (Zadok), *126, 127
Persons Attracted by the Form of the Mountain, 80, *85
Persons in the Presence of a Metamorphosis, *87
Philadelphia Museum of Art, see *Dog Barking at the Moon; Man, Woman, and Child; Nude; Person in the Presence of Nature*
Picasso, Pablo, 7, 19, 24, 28, 58, 111, 118; *Guernica*, 80, 86, *88
Picasso, Pablo, collection, see *Portrait of a Spanish Dancer; Self Portrait* (1919)
The Poetess, 106, *107
Portico, 135, *136
Portrait I, *95, 96
Portrait IV, *94, 96
Portrait of a Goldsmith, 14, *16
Portrait of Mrs. Mills in 1750, 60, 62, *63, 66
Portrait of J. F. Rafols, 14
Portrait of E. C. Ricart, 14, *15
Portrait of a Spanish Dancer, *31
The Potato, 58, *59
Prats, Joan, collection, see *Young Girl*

Raphael, *La Fornarina*, 60, *150
The Reaper, 88, *90, 91
The Red Disk in Pursuit of the Lark, 138, *144
Red Sun, *125, 127
Reynolds, Sir Joshua, 60
Rockefeller, Nelson, A., collection, see *"L'hirondelle d'amour"*
Roditi, Edouard, 23, 58, 149
Roméo et Juliette, designs for, 66, 149
Rope and People, *76
Rosengart, Siegfried, collection, see *"Amour"*
Rousseau, Henri, 24, 31, 32; *The Sleeping Gypsy*, 32

Saidenberg, Mr. and Mrs. Daniel, collection, see *Spanish Dancer*
Schoelkopf, Robert J., Jr., collection, see *"La Fornarina"*
sculpture, 9, *110, 111, 130, *135, *137
Seated Nude, 24, 26, *27, 31
Seated Woman, 66, *69
Self Portrait (1919), *26, 28
Self Portrait (1937–38), *92, 93, 96; later version of, 93
Sert, José Luis, 88
Sharp, Mrs. Evelyn, collection, see *Women Listening to Music*
Shoenberg, Mr. and Mrs. Sidney M., collection, see *Portrait of a Goldsmith*
Slifka, Mr. and Mrs. Joseph, collection, see *Standing Nude*
Smith, John R., 62
The Somersault, 39
Spain, Spanish, 19, 26, 32, 36, 38, 66, 80, 83, 87, 91, 124
Spanish Civil War, 31, 80, 83, 87, 88, 91
Spanish Dancer (Neumann), *61
Spanish Dancer, (Saidenberg), *116, 118
Standing Nude, *18, 26
Steen, Jan, *The Cat's Dancing Lesson*, *55, 58
Still Life with Old Shoe, 31, 80, 83, 86–87, 88, *89
Still Life with Rabbit, see *The Table*
Still Life with Toy Horse, *25
Sunyer, Ramón, 14; see also *Portrait of a Goldsmith*
Surrealism and surrealist, 7, 38–39, 45, 60, 86, 149
Sweeney, James Johnson, 7, 9, 55, 88, 100, 149, 150

The Table (Still Life with Rabbit), 28, *29
Table with Glove (Glove and Newspaper), 28, *30, 31
Tapestry, cartoon for, see *"L'hirondelle d'amour"*
Thompson, Mr. and Mrs. G. David, collection, *Painting; Portrait IV*
The Tilled Field, 36, *37, 45
Tjeder, Mrs. Hildegard Ault, collection, see *Woman and Kite* ...
A Toute Epreuve, 135, 137, 138, *139
Two Personages in Love with a Woman, *85

UNESCO murals, see *Day; Night* (mural)
Urgell Y Inglada, Modesto, 8–9, 10, 45; *Twilight*, *8, 9

Vase, *111
Vase of Flowers and Butterfly, *36
View of a Farm, 19, *20
View of Montroig (Alsdorf), *13
View of Montroig (Matisse Gallery), *12
The Village of Montroig, *22

Warner, Mr. and Mrs. Keith, collection, see *A Ballet Dancer* ...
Washington, D. C., The Phillips Gallery, see *Red Sun*
Watson, Peter, 91, 150
Weil, Mr. and Mrs. Richard K., collection, see *Nursery Decoration; Painting*
Werner, Theodor, collection, see *Composition*
Wiener, Mr. and Mrs. Paul Lester, collection, see *The Candle*
Winston, Mr. and Mrs. Donald, collection, see *Head of a Woman*
Winston, Mr. and Mrs. Harry Lewis, collection, see *Fratellini*
Woman, *78
Woman and Bird under the Moon, 106, *108
Woman and Bird in the Night, *114, 118
Woman and Birds in front of the Sun, 106, *109
Woman and Kite among the Constellations, *103
Woman and Little Girl in front of the Sun, *119, 120
Women by the Lake with an Iridescent Surface, after the Passage of a Swan, *105
Women Listening to Music, *112, 118
Women in the Night, *117, 120
Women at Sunrise, *120
Woodcuts, 135, 137, 138; see also *A Toute Epreuve*
World War II, 8, 93, 100
Wounded Personage, *104

Young Girl, *24

Zadok, Mr. and Mrs. Charles, collection, see *The Moon; Personages in the Night*
Zeisler, Dr. and Mrs. Ernest, collection, see *Wounded Personage*
Zervos, Christian, 66, 149
Zumsteg, Gustav M., see *The Table*